ONE WEEK
LOAN

THE HOWARD LEAGUE'S
GOOD PRACTICE GUIDE ON
**WORKING WITH
YOUNG OFFENDERS**

THE HOWARD LEAGUE'S GOOD PRACTICE GUIDE ON WORKING WITH YOUNG OFFENDERS

Bellew Publishing, London

Acknowledgements

A special thank you must go to Pauline Owen for researching and producing the first drafts of this report, and to Mike Grewcock for his contribution to the report writing. Thanks should also be passed to Bridget Gardiner who undertook some of the research in the North East of the country, and to Barry Hope and Save the Children Fund for allowing her to take the time to undertake this. The Howard League is also grateful to Hampshire Social Services who allowed Pauline Owen to be seconded for six months, and also to Hampshire Northern Youth Justice Unit who provided her with an office and plenty of encouragement.

The Howard League wishes to thank the Trustees of the Hayward Foundation and the Violet and Milo Cripps Charitable Trust for their generous support in funding the research for this book.

First published in Great Britain in 1994 by
Bellew Publishing Company Limited
8 Balham Hill, London SW12 9EA

ISBN 1 85 725 104 0

Typeset in the UK by Antony Gray
Printed and bound by
Hartnolls Ltd, Bodmin, Cornwall

Contents

Foreword　　7
by Andrew Rutherford, Chair of the Howard League

Glossary　　8

Preface　　9

Acknowledgements

Introduction　The Failings of Care and Custody　　11
Sentencing policy for young people – Inter-agency co-operation –
Clear policy and practice guidelines

1　Dealing with an Arrest　　19
Protecting vulnerable suspects – Kent Appropriate Adults
Scheme –Sandwell Youth Justice Unit: 24-hour PACE team –
Appropriate adults: a checklist for good practice

2　Diversion and Cautioning　　27
Background – Cautioning practice – Hampshire Youth Justice
Service – Devon and Cornwall Constabulary – Northampton &
West Yorkshire Liaison Bureau – Bromley Multi-agency
Cautioning Panel

3　Working in Court　　42
The provision of information – Solihull Youth Justice Centre –
Preparation for court hearings – Pre-trial visits: The Himmat
Project, Halifax – Support in court

4　Using the Bail Act　　47
The Bail Act 1976 – Bail information schemes – East Sussex
Probation Service – Bail support schemes – Surrey Bail Support
Scheme – Bail Out Support Scheme (BOSS), Southend –
Dover Bail Hostel

5　Avoiding prison remands　　67
Policy considerations – Start Point, S. Devon Social Services and
the Children's Society – South Glamorgan Remand Panel –
Kirklees Remand Fostering Scheme –
Young Offender Community Support Team, Fareham –
Headstart, Hertfordshire PACT

6 Community Sentences 92
*The supervision order: Surrey Youth Justice Scheme –
Supervision orders with specified activity orders – Hampshire
Youth Justice Service – Solihull Community Supervision –
Community service orders – The probation order – The
Kingsbury Project – The Himmat Project – The probation order
with conditions – The Edge Project, Leeds – Sherborne House –
Break-Free (The Haringey Project) – Lewisham and Greenwich
Intensive Probation Project – Hereford and Worcester Probation
Service: PACT – Geese Theatre Company – Devon Probation
Service: Victim Burglar Group – Kent Probation Service: The
Medway Centre*

7 Motor Projects 167
*Bradford Motor Project – Ilderton Motor project: South
London – Theatre Adad – Kent Auto Offenders' Scheme*

8 Partnerships 183
*Partnership arrangements with the voluntary sector –
Hampshire Youth Justice Service – Kent Youth Justice Service –
The Contract Project, County Durham – The growing
importance of the voluntary sector*

9 Conclusion 194
*Crime wave or moral panic? – The declining number of known
offenders – The nature of young offending – The proven failure of
approved schools – The development of
non-custodial options – The need for an overall strategy*

References 203

Legislation 203

About the Howard League 205

Foreword

The remarkable deceleration and humanising of youth justice that occurred in England and Wales during the 1980s was, to a large extent, brought about by practitioners. It was at the local level of practice that a rich variety of initiatives set the pace for national policy. Practitioners were able to demonstrate that not only can effective ways of working with young people be created and sustained but that the decision-making process of youth justice can be transformed.

Pauline Owen, the author of this book, was herself a key figure in these developments, both as a highly innovative practitioner and a leading figure in the Association for Juvenile Justice (as it then was). First-hand experience of this kind gives special authority to this compendium which will serve as an invaluable guide for all those concerned to work effectively with young people in trouble.

The Howard League commissioned this book in 1992, which was a time when the challenge ahead seemed to be largely one of building upon the achievements of the previous decade. However, in the months since the autumn of 1992 not only have the goal posts been moved by government ministers but a whole new ball game is underway. 'Back to basics' in its application to young offenders appears to promise a return to the 1950s when the police only rarely used their cautioning powers and young teenagers were packed off to distant and chilling institutions.

This timely book will make it all the more difficult to erase from political memory the considerable progress that has been made at the level of youth justice programmes. Pauline Owen has also provided a unique record of specific projects around the country which should do much to enhance dissemination of excellence in youth justice work. The Howard League is most grateful not only to Pauline Owen but to the many people who have assisted her in the publication of this handbook.

Andrew Rutherford
Chair of the Howard League, 1994

Glossary of Terms

CJA   Criminal Justice Act

CPS   Crown Prosecution Service

IT   Intermediate Treatment

Juvenile   Criminal justice arrangements dealing with children aged 17 and under.

Juvenile Court Prior to the CJA 1991, the majority of children aged 16 and under were dealt with by Juvenile Courts. The CJA 1991 dictated that 17 year olds should be included within the remit of new Youth Courts.

PSR   Pre-sentence report. A pre-sentence report is a report in writing, made or submitted by a probation officer or a social worker with a view to assisting the court in determining the most suitable method of dealing with an offender. Under the CJA 1991, a PSR must be considered before custody or certain more demanding community sentences are imposed. In addition, a PSR may be of value in advising the court about suitability for community sentences for which a PSR is not required by law, and in seeking to ensure that supervision, if ordered, is able to start promptly and effectively.

SIR   Social inquiry report. The SIR was superseded by the PSR in the 1991 Criminal Justice Act.

SOVA   Society of Voluntary Associates

YOI   Young Offender Institution

Youth Court see juvenile court above

Preface

This book was devised in 1992 in response to the damaging consequences of custody, especially the increasing number of suicides and acts of self-injury within the prison system. Forty-one people killed themselves in prison in 1992, including seven young men aged between 17 and 20. During that year there were also 2,872 recorded incidents of deliberate self-harm, 1,352 of which involved 968 different young people aged 20 and under.

Between August 1991 and March 1992, four young men aged between 15 and 20 hanged themselves while in custody at the Feltham Young Offender Institution and Remand Centre in Middlesex. Following these deaths, the Howard League established an independent inquiry into Feltham chaired by Anthony Scrivener QC and continued to campaign for the end of custodial penalties for juveniles.

In October 1992, the Home Secretary, Kenneth Clarke, signalled the re-introduction of approved schools for 12–14 year olds. This was despite the Home Office's own figures showing that incarceration in such institutions increases the likelihood of re-offending and in apparent disregard of what was learned during the 1980s.

During that decade, there was an encouraging shift away from the use of custody for young people culminating in the implementation of the Criminal Justice Act 1991 in October 1992. This coincided with the development of a wide range of non-custodial projects for young offenders in both the statutory and voluntary sectors.

These developments have been largely overlooked in the present 'public debate' over juvenile offending and are barely mentioned by Mr Clarke's successor, Michael Howard.

The underlying argument of this book is that a great deal of ground has been gained at the level of practice with young people. The book provides information on many of the non-custodial projects operating throughout England and Wales and aims to show that much useful work has been done to reduce the use of custody and offending amongst young people.

The book also aims to be a compendium of good practice, providing examples of schemes which could be established in all parts of the country and which may also be suitable for adults. Many of these schemes have been established with the active support of magistrates and court officials and it is hoped that this practical guide will assist the continuation of that trend.

A number of projects were visited during the preparation of this book. Time and space prevented them all from being covered. However, we are indebted to all those who have helped, particularly given that they were busy coping with the tremendous changes resulting from the introduction of the Criminal Justice Act 1991.

Changes in policy and practice arising from the Act have been included where possible. However, there are a number of omissions – most notably, services for mentally ill people and those charged with sexual offences.

The crime prevention aspects of some of the projects have also been left out, although some general aspects of crime prevention are discussed in the introduction.

Race and gender issues were given special attention throughout the research. The results have been patchy. Few projects were able to offer concrete examples of how to tackle racism. However, two projects did stand out – the Himmat Project in Halifax and the Edge Project in Leeds.

Introduction

The Failings of Care and Custody

Case Study: Craig Walsh, aged 15

When Craig Walsh was 10 years old, the teachers at his local school in Stoke-on-Trent complained they could not get him to listen or learn in class. He was sent to a local boarding school for difficult children, was unable to re-settle into normal school when he returned home two years later and began disappearing from home for days at a time. Social Services then placed Craig in a local hostel and, after various care placements during which time he became involved in minor offending, he was sent to a secure unit at Aycliffe from where he absconded after only a week. He was then sent to the Glenthorne Youth Treatment Centre in Birmingham.

Craig was a difficult boy with a lot of problems but he was also talented and caring. His parents spent many hours travelling to see him at Glenthorne where he developed gardening and sailing skills, even giving up a week-end trip to Alton Towers so that he could teach some handicapped children to sail.

However, Craig and another boy absconded one night and made their way back to Stoke. Under the influence of alcohol, they robbed Craig's aunt at knifepoint. They were arrested and held at Leek Police Station for several days during which time Craig cut his wrists.

Craig was remanded to Glen Parva Young Offender Institution with his Social Services file marked 'at risk of self-harm'. He remained on remand for two and a half months before being sentenced to thirty months detention. Three days after being sentenced, Craig again cut his wrists. The doctor who treated him recommended that Craig be placed in a shared cell but, contrary to prison regulations, this did not happen. Craig remained alone in a dingy cell for hours on end. His only furniture was a bunk bed, a table and two chairs. Supervision was minimal and association limited to 2–3 hours per day.

Repeated attempts to remove Craig from the prison system failed. In October 1990, he was found hanging in his prison cell. He was 15 years old.

The tragic case of Craig Walsh illustrates the shortcomings of the care system. Here was a vulnerable young boy who had

difficulty responding to the institutional solutions to his behaviour problems. He became enmeshed in a cycle of offending
and lashing out at those closest to him. He was a victim of a
totally inadequate suicide-prevention policy and a prison
regime utterly incapable of addressing the specialist needs of
difficult and troubled adolescents.

Prisons only serve to dehumanise the young people they
house. Due to the geographical isolation of the majority of
young offender institutions young people are often sent to
custody miles from their home communities, isolated from
their families and support. This was certainly the case for 15-
year-old Jeffrey Horler whose mother could not make the 200-
mile round trip to visit him in Feltham where he was to take
his own life.

The appalling conditions and poor provisions only compound the bleak nature of the prison experience. The young
men who spoke to members of the Howard League's Feltham
inquiry highlighted the desolating nature of life in custody:

'The beds are thin uncomfortable mattresses laid on metal
slats. You can't sleep on something like that even if you're
not constantly worried.'

'We need more association . . . one day you get 22.5 hours
locked in your cell, the second day its 23 hours locked in
your cell. Its terrible. If you're in here on your own like this,
I'm frightened that I'm going to be here for too long I'm not
going to be the same person when I leave.'

'I'd feel suicidal and scratched my arms with a battery case .
. . I can cut myself and just sit there . . . Its not deep enough
to do any damage but I can just sit there and watch the
blood dripping out. It feels as if all the pressure that's built
up inside me escapes through the cuts.'

The Howard League believes that locking children up brutal-
ises them and in the end adds to the crime problem. The
evidence of effectiveness demonstrates that prison does not
work. Young offender institutions like Feltham and Glen Parva
have extremely high failure rates: 80 per cent of the boys aged

15 and 16 on sentence who left custody in 1986 were reconvicted within two years of release. 62 per cent of boys aged 17 to 20 committed further offences over the same period. Locking up children virtually ensures that they re-offend. The horror stories and high re-conviction rates are repeated with secure accommodation. It does not matter what you use to lock them up; it all fails. Only very, very few young people need secure accommodation and that should be of the highest standard with committed, trained and well-paid staff.

The challenge of this book is to make sure that appropriate schemes are set up all over the country so that the courts never have to incarcerate children who can end up taking their own lives in prison. Not every case will end as sadly as that of Craig Walsh but the damaging effect of custody on both the young person and the community must be a key consideration for sentencers.

Sentencing policy for young people

In 1988, the Home Office published a Green Paper, *Punishment, Custody and the Community*, which stated:

... most young offenders grow out of crime as they become more mature and responsible. They need encouragement and help to become law-abiding. Even a short period of custody is quite likely to confirm them as criminals, particularly as they acquire new criminal skills from more sophisticated offenders. They see themselves labelled as criminals and behave accordingly.

This Green Paper laid the ground for the introduction of the Criminal Justice Act 1991 which marked a shift away from the use of custody for young people.

Section 1(2) of the Act, said that a Court should not pass a custodial sentence unless it is of the opinion

(a) that the offence or combination of the offence and one other offence associated with it is so serious that only such a sentence can be justified for the offence, or

(b) where the offence is a violent or sexual offence, that only such a sentence would be adequate to protect the public from serious harm.

The Criminal Justice Act 1993 back-tracked on this by amending the earlier Act so that Section 1 (2) now reads:

... that the offence, or combination of the offence and one or more offences associated with it, was so serious that only such a sentence can be justified for the offence ...

As the following chart shows, the Youth and Crown Courts currently (1993) have the power to impose a wide range of community-based sentences on juveniles:

Age	Sentence Available
10–13 years	Absolute discharge
	Conditional discharge
	Bind over of offender or parents
	Fine (for which parent can be made responsible)
	Compensation order (for which parent can be made responsible)
	Attendance centre order
	Supervision order
	Supervision order with requirement including:
	o psychiatric treatment
	o educational requirements
	o night restriction requirements
	o specified activities
	o residence requirements
	Detention under S.53 Children and Young Persons Act 1933 for murder or manslaughter
14 years	All of the above
	Detention under S.53 for offences for which an adult could receive 14 years or more imprisonment
15 years	All of the above
	Detention in a Young Offender Institution for up to 12 months

16–17 years   All of the above, plus
Probation order
Probation order with:
- residence requirement
- activity requirement
- probation centre requirement
- mental treatment requirement
- requirement of treatment for drug or alcohol dependency

Community Service Order
Combination Order
Detention under S.53 for offence of indecent assault on a woman

During his speech to the 1993 Conservative Party Conference, Michael Howard, the Home Secretary, announced proposals to introduce or amend the following sanctions:

- to introduce a new Secure Training Order for up to two years for persistent juvenile offenders aged 12 to 14 years;
- to double the maximum custodial sentence in a Young Offender Institution for 15 to 17 year olds from one to two years.

Inter-agency co-operation
The alternative programmes Probation and Social Services Departments can offer will often determine which sentencing option is implemented. There is considerable variation in the range and quality of youth justice services depending on how these were developed when the shift away from youth custody was established during the 1980s.

Probation and Social Services Departments are now required by the Criminal Justice Act 1991 to have a joint approach to the management of services for 16 and 17 year olds.

In addition, Home Office Circular 30/92 requires chief officers from both Probation and Social Services to ensure a local method for the planning of services to the Youth Court in order 'to make the best use of opportunities and resources for constructive work with offenders in this age group and to avoid conflicts in objectives and working methods, duplication of effort, or failure to provide necessary support'. The circular further states that the local Justices' Clerk will play a part in ensuring such arrangements are being made.

The Children Act 1989 also introduced a duty upon local authorities to encourage juveniles within their area not to commit offences. This duty is to be discharged in a corporate manner, i.e., involving the full range of resources available to the local authority. The guidance notes for the implementation of the Children Act suggest each authority establishes a standing committee on juvenile crime with representatives from all the agencies concerned with young people who are likely to offend.

Local practitioners feel more confident about dealing with the small numbers of very demanding young people if local planning on youth crime has existed for some time in the area. Combining resources means that more options are available and encourages an atmosphere of wanting to explore every option.

Two characteristics stand out in those areas where joint plans between Probation and Social Services are well established. Firstly, chief officers are committed to services for young people and are prepared to fight for the necessary funding and resources; secondly, much of the key decision-making is delegated to senior managers.

However, shortages of funds and tensions between the various agencies have hindered the development of joint plans in some areas.

Clear policy and practice guidelines

Successful joint schemes require a clearly stated policy with written procedures and practice guidelines. These provide a young person with a clear understanding of his/her responsibilities, they provide the professionals in the field with consistent targets and work practices and give the courts a consistent service upon which they can rely.

Over the past ten years, the following principles have merged to underpin such policies:

1. adolescence is a period of rapid physical and emotional change, characterised by insecurity and experimental behaviour;
2. offending is a common occurrence during adolescence;
3. juvenile offending is often transitory in nature with most young people maturing out of it. The peak age of offending is between 16 and 18 years;
4. the majority of juvenile crime is not serious in nature and represents a nuisance rather than a danger to the public;
5. bringing young people into the criminal justice system at too early an age contributes to re-offending;
6. the normal institutions of family, school and community are positively associated with the process of maturing;
7. removal from home into institutions will often harden attitudes to offending and retard maturing;
8. the small number of young people who persist in offending may require intensive forms of supervision in which the court has confidence;
9. all young people are entitled to an equal opportunity of service, regardless of race, sex or disability;
10. the use of custody for young people has proved an ineffective response to youth crime. High re-conviction rates from custodial institutions illustrate that custodial sanctions rarely rehabilitate the offender.

Principles like these have shaped two forms of intervention by youth criminal justice workers in recent years.

The first is known as 'proportionate intervention'. It involves targeting specific young people who require social work support and specific aspects of their offending behaviour. It can be distinguished from the blanket approach, common throughout the 1970s, of aiming to attach a social worker to every young person who offends.

The research of Thorpe (1980) and Rutherford (1992) shows how this earlier blanket approach did not work. It can be contrasted with the experience of the early 1980s when proportionate intervention methods were successfully used in a number of intermediate treatment schemes.

The second, related form of intervention is known as 'systems intervention'. It involves conscious intervention by criminal justice agencies at specific stages of the criminal justice process – for example, the multi-agency schemes discussed in chapter two which deal with cautioning young people.

Examples of both forms of intervention are discussed in the following chapters.

Chapter 1

Dealing with an Arrest

Protecting vulnerable suspects
Police powers of arrest and detention are governed by the Police and Criminal Evidence Act 1984 (PACE). The Codes of Practice accompanying the Act outline the procedures which the police must follow and define the roles of other professionals, such as social workers and youth justice officers.

Part C of the Codes is designed to protect vulnerable suspects and to ensure that interviews conducted by the police will be regarded as safe by the courts.

Who is vulnerable?

○ any person under the age of 17;
○ someone with learning difficulties or who cannot read or write;
○ someone suffering from a mental illness;
○ a person who is blind, deaf or unable to speak.

How are they protected?
A vulnerable suspect must be accompanied by an appropriate adult. In the case of a juvenile, the Act describes this person as:

i   a parent or guardian (or if s/he is in care, the care authority or organisation);
ii   a social worker; or
iii another responsible adult who is not a police officer or employed by the police.

It cannot be the solicitor or legal adviser.
   The appropriate adult should:

○ advise the detained person and ensure that s/he understands any legal advice;
○ observe that interviews and other procedures are carried out fairly;

- safeguard the rights of the detained person;
- participate in an active manner.

For any young person, being arrested and taken to a police station can be an intimidating and bewildering experience. This also applies to parents, especially if they are angry or embarrassed and have never had to deal with such a situation before.

The police must always inquire whether one of the parents or the guardian will act as an appropriate adult.

Who can substitute for the parents?
Some areas provide specialist youth justice staff if a parent is unavailable or unwilling to attend.

Difficulties can arise if such specialist services do not exist. There is a temptation for police and solicitors to put convenience ahead of the rights of the vulnerable person by accepting appropriate adults who cannot effectively discharge their responsibilities.

This puts a young person at a disadvantage in the face of hostile questioning or pressure to accept an allegation which may not be true.

Here are some examples of schemes which attempt to provide an appropriate adult service.

Kent Appropriate Adult Scheme

Social Services, Kent County Council, I.Q.A. (Inspection, Quality, Assurance), Springfield, Maidstone, Kent ME14 2LW
Telephone: Maidstone (0622) 671411

This scheme is run by a local voluntary organisation, the Council for Social Responsibility, on behalf of the Social Services Department.

Volunteers are given basic training about PACE and young people and attempts are being made to improve representation amongst ethnic minorities. The scheme co-ordinator is a volunteer who can be contacted if the police require an appropriate adult after hours.

The co-ordinator has the following duties:

- ○ arranging the attendance of appropriate adults at police stations;
- ○ recruiting and overseeing the training of volunteers;
- ○ attending the inter-agency liaison group on PACE;
- ○ monitoring the activities of the scheme;
- ○ providing an annual evaluation of the scheme.

The Scheme is overseen and assisted by a liaison group comprising representatives from the police, Social Services and the Council for Social Responsibility.

The Scheme does not provide volunteers if the child is already in care or has a social worker.

Results

During 1991, the Scheme was used on 376 occasions.

The reasons for needing such a scheme are illustrated by the figures for Kent for the period 1 November 1991 to 31 January 1992:

Reason	Number	%
Parents refused to attend	15	27.8
Foster parent unwilling	2	3.7
Parents/carers unable to attend	18	33.4
Police unable to contact parents	1	1.8
Parents/family – victims	5	9.3
Parents also arrested	3	5.6
No contact with parents	1	1.8
Parents not wanted by juvenile	2	3.7
Reason unclear	7	12.9
Totals	**54**	**100.0**

Sandwell Youth Justice Unit: 24-hour PACE team

Sandwell Youth Justice Unit, Charlemont, Pennyhill Lane, West Bromwich, Sandwell, West Midlands B71 3RY
Telephone: (021) 588 8325

This team consists of four staff – two team managers and two social workers. Each member of the team receives specific training in the duties of the appropriate adult. Its duties are as follows:

○ to provide a 24-hour response to police requests for an appropriate adult;
○ to ensure a minimum delay in responding;
○ to reduce the time juveniles spend in custody;
○ to advise and assist detained juveniles in accordance with their rights under PACE;
○ to ensure the PACE codes are followed;
○ to ensure that the Sandwell Youth Justice Team is aware of potentially difficult cases as soon as possible.

The team is based at a residential children's home which provides accommodation for young people on remand. When not required by the police, team members work as back-up staff in the home.

The scheme has several advantages:

○ it provides a consistent, high-quality service which can be relied upon by detained young people and the police;
○ delays and unnecessary periods of detention are reduced;
○ team members are more familiar with local authority services and available alternative accommodation.

Parental involvement at the earliest possible stage can facilitate a young person being sent home rather than placed on remand. This highlights the need for appropriate adults to supply the parents with helpful information as soon as possible.

As the following figures show, much juvenile offending is done after hours. There is therefore a problem if the police turn to a PACE team rather than spend time contacting a parent.

The following table shows interviews attended by Sandwell PACE team during 1991:

Time	Number
after 5 pm	178
9 am to 5 pm	82
pre 5 pm to post 5 pm	4
Total	**264**

General Advantages

The existence of a dedicated PACE team means a young person's interests can be protected by someone with experience and understanding of the local police.

Specialist teams are less likely to be distracted by other work pressures. This is particularly important if the young person is in care. Many social workers and residential workers do not have a thorough knowledge of PACE, nor the time to attend lengthy interviews.

Figures for Peterborough in Cambridgeshire provide an indication of the amount of time that can be consumed by appropriate adult duties. In 1991, appropriate adults were required in Peterborough on 167 occasions for an average of 2–4 hours each, leading to a weekly average of 15 hours.

The attendance breakdown was:

- 34% juveniles in care;
- 27% parents unwilling to attend;
- 10% parents unable to attend because of language problems; and
- 29% parents attended.

Experience shows that where PACE teams exist, they get used. They can provide important protection for a young person and can avoid lengthy delays for all parties at the police station.

Case Study: 'George'

At 3 pm, the police phoned the Juvenile Justice Unit to say that George, a 16 year old known to them already, had been arrested. They also provided information regarding the time of arrest, the circumstances, attempts to contact the parents and the fact that George had declined the offer of a solicitor. They said they were ready to interview in 30 minutes.

The youth justice officer agreed to attend the interview and registered concern at the fact that George had been in custody for over 4 hours. George's solicitors were contacted immediately and agreed to attend the police station at 3.45pm

Both the solicitor and the appropriate adult were present at 3.45pm but, after waiting for some time and making three inquiries, were told the interviewing officers could not be found.

The appropriate adult requested the custody officer be told that the delay was denying George his right to legal advice. He was not being dealt with 'diligently and expeditiously' as required by PACE. In effect, he was being held incommunicado. After two minutes, the solicitor and appropriate adult were shown into the cell block.

The custody officer confirmed that George was only under arrest for one offence. George then had a private consultation with his solicitor and the appropriate adult. He decided to admit the offence as he had been caught in the act. He was then formally interviewed for about five minutes during which time he explained the circumstances of the offence to the officers.

Just as it appeared the interview was to end, one of the interviewing officers produced a file containing details of a number of burglaries and said: 'Now George, you have been very co-operative so far, I want to talk to you about some other matters.' At this point, both the solicitor and the appropriate adult intervened to say that George was not under arrest for these other matters and asked whether there was sufficient evidence to arrest him for them. They pointed out that if there was sufficient evidence, he should have been arrested before the interview started or when the custody officer originally authorised detention.

The police asserted that they had the right to ask as many questions as they liked. The appropriate adult responded that this was a breach of S.31 of PACE which prevents abuse of the time limits for detention in police custody without charge.

The interview was terminated forthwith and George was arrested for one of the additional burglaries. The appropriate adult insisted that the custody officer record the concerns about the failure to comply with section 31 in the custody record and extracted a written acknowledgment that, at the time, the police did not have sufficient evidence to arrest George for any of the remaining offences.

George had a further consultation with his solicitor and the appropriate adult and, on advice, exercised his right to silence throughout the following interview.

George was released on bail for both the offence he had admitted and the outstanding matter. He was eventually cautioned for the first offence with no further action on the second after the police decided against convening an identification parade.

Appropriate adults – a checklist for good practice

1. The appropriate adult should be familiar with the Police and Criminal Evidence Act and understand the expectations imposed by the Act and its regulations.
2. The appropriate adult's role is actively to ensure fairness during the interview.
3. The appropriate adult should establish why the parents cannot be present, whether they know the child is in custody and assist with transport if required.
4. The appropriate adult should establish whether the young person has special language needs, communication problems or mental illness.
5. The police should provide an interpreter if English is not the detained person's first language.
6. The appropriate adult should check the time of detention with the police and agree meal breaks and periods of rest and exercise. The appropriate adult should also check the cell is adequately heated and that the young person has adequate clothes.
7. The appropriate adult should check the young person understands his/her rights. Can the young person paraphrase them?
8. The appropriate adult should ensure the young person has been given access to legal advice. This includes ensuring proper consultation prior to interview and, if necessary, delaying interviews to enable this to happen.
9. During the interview, the seating positions should allow the solicitor and the appropriate adult to offer full support.
10. The young person must be able to understand the questions and the implications of any answers.

11. Police should not be allowed to ask the same question repeatedly, badger the detained person or engage in verbal intimidation.
12. The solicitor and the appropriate adult should ask to check the custody record.
13. There is a particular need to deal with young people expeditiously and to ensure their release as soon as possible.

Chapter 2

Diversion and Cautioning

Background

Cautioning is recognised as an increasingly important way of keeping offenders out of the courts and, in many circumstances, out of further trouble.   Home Office Circular 59/90

The police have a wide choice of options for dealing with young people. They can:

o   take no further action;
o   give an informal warning on the street;
o   give an informal warning at the police station;
o   give an instant caution;
o   give a caution after consultation with other agencies;
o   give a caution after consultation and refer for support;
o   initiate proceedings.

Cautioning is an effective way of diverting many young people involved in only minor offending from experiencing the full weight of the criminal justice system. It is important that this diversion occurs as early as possible as it is widely recognised that young people who become involved in the judicial process are more likely to re-offend.

Cautioning has been used extensively with young people and has been largely seen as a success. In 1990, 70% of male and 86% of female offenders aged 14 to 16 were cautioned by the police.

Much of the recent publicity concerning young people has attempted to highlight those who have been repeatedly cautioned. Home Office Circular 59/90 impels senior police officers to 'bear in mind the danger that inappropriate use of cautioning, especially repeat cautioning, might undermine the credibility of the police and ultimately the law'.

Multiple cautioning is not generally widespread. A sample

study of juveniles cautioned in a one-week period in November 1991 shows that just 3% had two or more cautions:

Previous cautioning history of juveniles cautioned in the week 25–29 November 1991 (parliamentary answer by Michael Jack, 26.2.92)

Police Force Area	% of previous cautions				
	0	1	2	more than 2	Total*
Metropolitan	57	24	10	9	100
South Wales	73	15	6	6	100
Gt. Manchester	77	17	4	3	101
Merseyside	79	17	3	-	99
West Midlands	82	11	4	4	101
West Yorkshire	69	21	8	1	99
Northumbria	75	15	10	-	100
All police forces	73	16	8	3	100

*Totals may not equal 100%

This confirms earlier studies of juveniles cautioned in 1985 and 1988 which found that 84% and 75% respectively had no previous cautions (Home Office Statistical Bulletin 20/92).

The Howard League recently pointed out that 'in any event, multiple cautions should not be seen as a failure on the part of those cautioned or the cautioning practice itself. Custody is repeatedly used despite its poor results in deterring youngsters from re-offending. Only 20–30% of young people sent to prison do not re-offend within 2 years of release' (1993).

The use of cautioning increased during the 1980s as its value in reducing re-offending rates became widely accepted. However, at the time of writing, a new draft circular on cautioning had been issued on 29.10.1993 which stipulates that:

. . . cautions should never be used for the most serious indictable-only offences such as attempted murder or rape, and only in the most exceptional circumstances for other indictable-only offences, regardless of the age or previous record of the offender.

With regard to repeat cautioning the draft goes on:

It is only in exceptional circumstances that more than one caution should be considered. This would be:

o where the subsequent offence is more minor and of a different nature from the first; or
o where there has been an appreciable lapse of time since the last offence.

The effect of this tougher line on cautioning is not yet apparent as this book goes to print.

Nevertheless, the purpose of cautioning is outlined in Home Office Circular 59/90 as:

o to deal quickly and simply with less serious offenders;
o to divert them from the criminal courts; and
o to reduce their chances of re-offending.

Three conditions must be satisfied before a caution is administered:

o there must be sufficient evidence of the offender's guilt to give a realistic prospect of conviction;
o the offender must admit the offence; and
o a juvenile's parents must give informed consent.

Circular 59/90 lists the factors to be taken into account including:

o the nature of the offence;
o the likely penalty;
o the offender's age and state of health;
o the offender's criminal history;
o the offender's attitude towards the offence; and
o the victim's view of the offence.

There is a presumption in favour of not prosecuting juveniles and other vulnerable groups.

Cautioning practice
Although Home Office circular 59/90 makes recommendations about how cautioning decisions should be made, conflicting views amongst the professionals involved can often

Hampshire's Youth Justice System and Gatekeeping

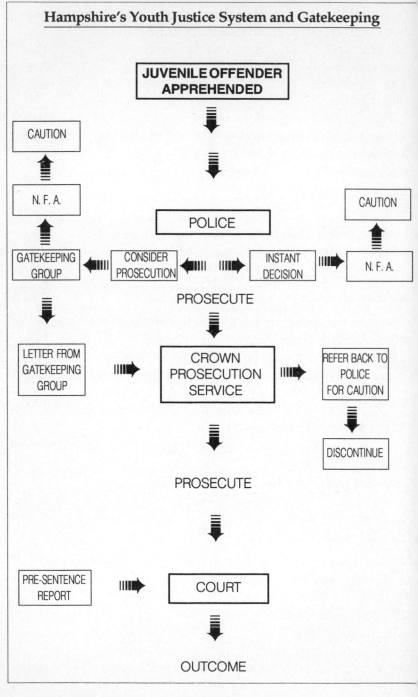

present difficulties for inter-agency cautioning schemes. Variations between and within police force areas are still common. In some areas, cautions are administered on the basis that young people will automatically receive social work services. The varying degrees of justice and due process can literally mean 'justice by geography'.

This chapter looks at four examples of cautioning schemes. All four involve close liaison between youth justice workers and the local police. Three are specifically designed for young people under 18.

Hampshire Youth Justice Service

North Hants Juvenile Justice Unit, Woodlands Centre,
180 Culver Road, Basingstoke RG21 3NL
Telephone: Basingstoke (0256) 464034/20766

South East Hants Juvenile Justice Unit

Darby House, Southwick Hill Road, Cosham,
Portsmouth PO6 3LU
Telephone: Porstmouth (0705) 370013

South West Hants Juvenile Justice Unit

33 Selborne Avenue, Harefield, Southampton SO2 5DZ
Telephone: Southampton (0703) 463336

Background

This cautioning scheme was established in 1987 by the Hampshire Youth Justice System which has always placed great importance on good liaison with the police. It operates as part of a formal process, commonly known as a 'gatekeeping system', designed to keep as many young people out of the court system as possible. There are three local offices, each of which has established gatekeeping groups for the police subdivisions within their catchment area.

How it works

There are fortnightly meetings between Youth Justice Service staff, the police (usually an inspector), social workers and

Education Service managers. These consider all young people under the age of 18 whom the police are recommending for prosecution.

As can be seen from its prosecution policy detailed below, unlike some areas, the Hampshire Constabulary has a policy on prosecution rather than cautioning.

The preferred method to institute proceedings against persons under the age of 18, will be to report for process. By thus deferring a decision, the case may be considered at Gatekeeping meetings. Charging should not be used for those under the age of 14 years . . . a Custody Officer . . . **may** charge a person under the age of 18, either individually or jointly, with an offence in any of the following circumstances:

a) The offence is a serious offence (see below);
b) The young offender has been arrested for an offence on warrant;
c) The young offender is currently the resident of a community home or penal establishment and after consultation, usually by telephone, with the Juvenile Justice Unit, the latter has indicated that prosecution would be the most suitable course;
d) The young offender has previous findings of guilt for criminal offences in criminal courts on three or more separate and distinct occasions. If as a result of a recent court appearance the offender is still subject of a supervision or care order or other **known** Social Services or Juvenile Justice Unit's interest then it would be appropriate **not** to charge without consulting the Juvenile Justice Unit;
e) The offender is already due to appear in court for an alleged offence and an Inspector has authorised an additional charge.

from Hampshire Constabulary,
Prosecution Policy, September 1992

Decisions to prosecute are made on criteria relating to the

offence, not the personal circumstances of the individual concerned. This makes the administration of the gatekeeping and cautioning process easier for all to manage.

Each meeting is chaired by the Youth Justice Team manager. The police outline the basic details of the offence after which the team discusses its seriousness, whether or not the young person admits the offence, the young person's view of the offence, the impact of the offence on the victim and the offender and the merits of proceeding with a prosecution.

After each recommendation, the team manager completes an information form which accompanies the file back to the police and the Crown Prosecution Service. The form outlines any disagreements which may assist the CPS in deciding whether the case should continue.

The scale and nature of the work is illustrated by the Northern Youth Justice Unit situated at Basingstoke:

○ 6 police sub-divisions are covered;

○ 902 cases were considered in the 60 gatekeeping meetings of 1992;

○ on average, a case takes two weeks from the time of arrest to discussion at the gatekeeping meeting. Delays may occur if those at the meeting think more information is required to enable a decision to be made. Split decisions are recorded and the file passed to the CPS for a final decision;

○ young people and their parents do not attend these meetings but are informed about them after they are arrested or reported for summons.

Cautioning

The police decide whether there will be no further action or an informal warning. For those who have previously offended, the Hampshire Constabulary prosecution policy states:

Cautions for second or subsequent offences will only be precluded where the offence in question is so **serious** as to require prosecution. Previous cautions or findings of guilt, including those which have resulted in probation or supervision orders or conditional discharge, will not necessarily preclude a further caution which may be appropriate where:

a) there has been a significant lapse of time since the earlier offence; or
b) the current or earlier offence was trivial; or
c) the current offence is different in nature from the earlier offence.

Serious offences are:
a) homicide (including driving offences);
b) those involving gross personal violation (rape, sexual assaults upon children);
c) arson endangering life;
d) serious public disorder;
e) the supply of a class A controlled drug;
f) drink driving offences;
g) those in which significant harm has been done to a person;
h) those in which property of substantial value has been stolen or substantial damage has been caused.

An offence may also be serious depending upon the wilfulness with which harm or damage was done, or the degree of suffering caused to an individual.

Advantages of this approach
1) decisions are based on the nature of the offence, not the individual;
2) a standard policy limits bias by particular agencies and ensures consistency across a large county and inner city and rural areas;
3) the services require professional co-operation and are not dependent on the personalities of those involved;
4) young people who do not require a caution are not identified to the Youth Justice Service;
5) it demands a solid knowledge of the law from the Youth Justice Service and a proactive approach to working with the police; and
6) information is shared on a strictly 'need to know basis'.

Devon and Cornwall Constabulary

Chief Constables Office, Middlemoor, Exeter,
Devon EX2 7HQ
Telephone: Exeter (0392) 52101

Background

In order to provide consistency throughout a large police force area, the Devon and Cornwall Constabulary have negotiated with Probation, Social Services and the Crown Prosecution Service to produce practical guidelines and offence criteria for the operation of their diversion and cautioning programme. These guidelines have ensured that fewer inappropriate cases have gone to court, a more effective use of cautioning for all age groups and a professional streamlining of decision making to minimise individual prejudice or bias.

How it works

○ This is a gatekeeping system similar to that which operates in Hampshire.

○ The criteria are applied by the gatekeeping group to all offences considered capable of proof.

○ Each offence is accorded a number on a gravity scale of 1–5 with those ranked at 5 almost always being prosecuted. However, there is a specific scale of mitigating factors and each case is individually assessed. Co-defendants are treated separately and when multiple charges are laid, the most serious is considered.

Prosecution and Diversion Criteria used by Devon and Cornwall Constabulary for Disposal Decision

Gravity Score	Disposal
1	Warning (NFA detected)
2	High probability of caution; police decision-maker needs to be able to justify decision not to caution
3	Pivotal; the particular circumstances of offence or offender and any mitigating or aggravating factors,

will determine whether the disposal moves up or down.

4   High probability of prosecution; police decision-maker needs to be able to justify decision not to prosecute.

5   Will always be prosecuted; mitigating gravity factors are most unlikely to affect the decision to prosecute.

Detailed below are examples of how Devon and Cornwall Constabulary rate the gravity of the following offences.

Northampton and West Youth Liaison Bureau

OFFENCE		GRAVITY FACTORS	
CRIMINAL DAMAGE		**+ FACTORS**	**– FACTORS**
Criminal Damage (including arson) whereby life endangered	5		
Criminal Damage (including arson)	3	○ Damage deliberate rather than reckless ○ Potential of greater danger ○ Damage over £200	○ Damage under £50
Threat to destroy property of another	3	○ Potential value of damage over £200	○ Potential value of damage under £50
Possession of articles with intent to commit criminal damage	3	○ Evidence of intent to commit serious criminal damage ○ Potential value of damage over £200	○ Potential value of damage under £50
PUBLIC ORDER ACT 1986			
Riot (S.1.)	5		
Violent disorder (S.2.)	4		
Affray (S.3.)	4		
Threatening abusive or insulting words or behaviour intended to cause fear of violence or to provoke violence (S.4.)	3	○ Extent of concern felt by person affected ○ Risk of escalation	

Northampton and West Youth Liaison Bureau

The Diversion Unit, 198 Kettering Road,
Northampton NN1 4BL
Telephone (0604) 601241

Background

Here, there is a different approach from that of Devon and Cornwall.

In 1984, Northamptonshire Constabulary established its Youth Liaison Bureau, involving representatives from the police, Probation, Social Services, Education and youth work. It has a clear commitment to diverting as many young people as possible from the penal system.

The aims of the Bureau are outlined in Chapter eight. It reviews the cases of all offenders under 18 years and recommends a course of action to the police.

How it works

o   The Bureau offers specialist assistance to young people and their families. Referrals or information can be given on subjects such as safe driving, alcohol abuse and counselling.

o   An individual package can be provided for a young person who admits an offence. These packages are voluntary and may involve making an indirect or direct gesture of reparation or apology to the victim.

o   The Bureau gathers information which helps provide an accurate picture of the effects and patterns of youth crime.

o   As can be seen below, one of the Bureau's major successes has been an increased use of informal action for young people who would otherwise be subject to cautions or prosecution.

o   Care is also taken to avoid unduly intrusive social work intervention.

o   However, criminal justice agencies can react disproportionately when the above approach fails and the young person commits further offences.

Results

The Bureau's work highlights the general value of diverting

young people from the penal system. A recent Home Office study showed that 87% of juveniles cautioned in 1985 were not convicted of a further offence within the next two years. (Home Office Statistical Bulletin 20/92, 6.8.92; also see *Young and in Trouble*, Howard League, 1993.)

Northampton and West Youth Liaison Bureau: percentages of disposal 1986–91

	1986	1989	1991
No further action	11.60	19.50	15.06
Informal action	21.67	49.62	56.52
Caution	43.61	15.49	9.30
Written caution	4.98	2.82	2.49
Prosecution	23.12	12.57	16.31
Total non-prosecutions	81.86	87.43	83.37

*Totals may not equal 100%

Bromley Multi-agency Cautioning Panel

South East London Probation Service, Crosby House, 9/13 Elmfield Road, Bromley, Kent BR1 1LT
Telephone (081) 464 3430

Background
The special considerations which apply additionally to the young, the elderly and the infirm and other vulnerable groups will tend to mean that cautioning rates will remain higher for these groups than for others. But there is no reason why adults should be excluded from cautioning by reason only of their age.

(Home Office Circular 59/1990, *The Cautioning of Offenders*)

Despite the availability of cautions for those over 18, the figures indicate they are little used. The Bromley scheme aims to redress this imbalance by providing a system of cautioning for those aged 17 to 20.

It originated in 1989 when the South East London Probation Service and the Metropolitan Police initiated a multi-agency group involving FIRM (now Mediation Concern), the Society of

Voluntary Associates (SOVA), the Crown Prosecution Service, Bromley Magistrates Court, police and senior probation officers to review the implementation of the forthcoming Home Office Circular 59/1990.

The multi-agency group also instituted training for police officers, particularly custody sergeants, on the implementation of the cautioning guidelines in Home Office circular 59/1990.

A Young Offenders Panel was established for a 12-month pilot period in July 1991 and is still operating. It consists of representatives from SOVA, the police, the Probation Service, the Social Services criminal justice team and a chair or representative from the Police Consultative Committee with a quorum of representatives from SOVA, probation and the police.

How it works

The Young Offenders Panel considers the cases of young people for whom a caution may be appropriate. They must reside in the Borough of Bromley, admit the offence and give informed consent to a caution. Before consent is sought, there must be sufficient evidence to secure a conviction. The police reserve the right to charge immediately if the offence is triable only on indictment or is considered very serious.

The Panel also considers those not suitable for immediate charge or caution who admit the offence and agree to a referral.

Before each referral, the young person is contacted by a probation officer who provides a short, written assessment to the Panel. One of the following recommendations is then made to the police: charge, caution, caution with support or no further action.

If the Panel cannot reach agreement, the matter is referred back to the appropriate chief superintendent who makes the final decision.

The flow-chart overleaf was produced to enable the police to make consistent decisions based on the nature of the offending. A 'Caution Consideration Chart' is also implemented to assist custody sergeants decide whether an offence merits consideration of a caution. The chart provides information on how

Bromley Young Adults Cautioning System for 17–20 year olds

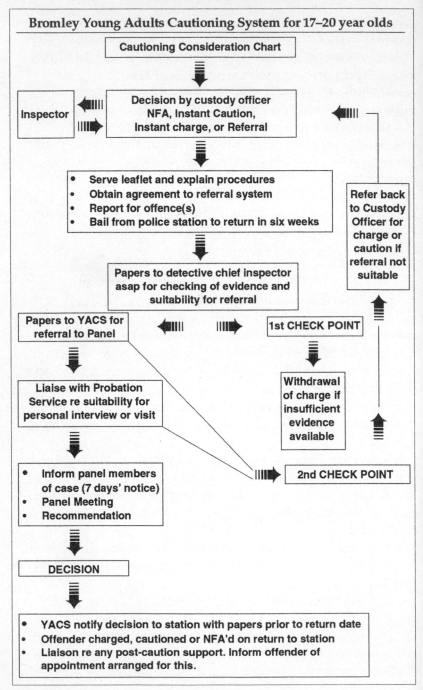

Cautioning Consideration Chart

Inspector

Decision by custody officer NFA, Instant Caution, Instant charge, or Referral

- Serve leaflet and explain procedures
- Obtain agreement to referral system
- Report for offence(s)
- Bail from police station to return in six weeks

Refer back to Custody Officer for charge or caution if referral not suitable

Papers to detective chief inspector asap for checking of evidence and suitability for referral

Papers to YACS for referral to Panel

1st CHECK POINT

Liaise with Probation Service re suitability for personal interview or visit

Withdrawal of charge if insufficient evidence available

- Inform panel members of case (7 days' notice)
- Panel Meeting
- Recommendation

2nd CHECK POINT

DECISION

- YACS notify decision to station with papers prior to return date
- Offender charged, cautioned or NFA'd on return to station
- Liaison re any post-caution support. Inform offender of appointment arranged for this.

policy has been translated into practice and general data on the scheme.

Each young adult wishing to participate in the Scheme is assessed and provided with an individual action plan, the aim of which is to address specific needs like accommodation, money problems or the constructive use of leisure time.

A SOVA volunteer is then linked in to work one to one with the young adult on a task-oriented and time-limited programme, using the local facilities and resources in the borough.

SOVA volunteers
SOVA has a conscious policy of recruiting volunteers from a wide variety of backgrounds. In 1991/92, SOVA recruited almost 300 volunteers of whom:

o   10% had criminal records;
o   14% were aged 18–24 years;
o   20% were aged 25–29 years;
o   63% were female and 37% male;
o   77% white European;
o   10% black Caribbean; and
o   4% were Asian.

SOVA volunteers undertook 29,000 hours of community work in 1991/92 involving a wide range of activities. These go well beyond the scope of the Bromley Cautioning Scheme and include literacy training, basic adult education, drug/alcohol awareness, HIV/AIDS awareness, accommodation and group leisure schemes.

Chapter 3

Working in Court

This chapter looks at the duties of the probation officer, social worker or youth justice worker in the courtroom. The examples are taken from the Youth Court but could also apply to adult courts.

Background
The Children Act 1989 removed civil proceedings from the Juvenile Court leaving it with an exclusively criminal jurisdiction.

The Criminal Justice Act 1991 replaced the Juvenile Court with the Youth Court and extended its jurisdiction to include 17 year olds. Juvenile panels became Youth Court panels.

Now, all children under 18 years who face criminal charges are subject to the principle set out in S.44 of the Children and Young Persons Act 1933, that all courts must have regard to the welfare of the children and young people who appear before them.

The Criminal Justice Act 1991 created an expectation that Probation and Social Services would work closely together in the design and management of services available to the Court.

This has led to the development of multi-agency teams specialising in youth justice work. The major advantage of such a team is that it is an identifiable service responsible for the majority of resources relevant to the court process: bail information, bail support, court duty, preparation of pre-sentence reports and the management of community penalties. The police retain management of attendance centres.

If such arrangements are not in place, social workers and probation officers can be working under different guidelines, with different expectations of magistrates and with the risk that some services will not be properly co-ordinated.

Part of the process of developing multi-agency teams is the

development of common principles of practice. These are often formulated with the assistance of magistrates and clerks and are generally in line with those set out in the *National Standards for the Supervision of Offenders*, jointly published by the Department of Health, the Home Office and the Welsh Office in August 1992.

This chapter looks at three areas of work within the Court. The provision of services in these areas is not well developed but, as the following examples show, there is a need to consider the particular problems young people face when thrown into the court system.

The provision of information

Solihull Youth Justice Centre

Solihull Juvenile Centre, 8 Craig Croft, Chelmsley Wood, Birmingham B37 7TR
Telephone: 021 7702534

The Solihull Juvenile Justice Unit was established as a specialist team by Solihull Social Services in 1987. All staff are qualified and experienced in a variety of techniques and practices to enable constructive, intensive and effective work to be undertaken with young people.

The Unit is assisted by the Community Support Team, a pool of twenty local people who are trained and supported to befriend and assist youngsters in the community, especially during the evenings and at weekends.

The Unit is based at the Solihull Juvenile Centre whose many services include providing young people and their families with basic information about the court process. *A Guide to Criminal Proceedings in Solihull Youth Court*, a pamphlet especially produced for young people and their parents, is shown overleaf as an example of the type of information provided.

The Centre explains to the young people and their families the role of each individual in the court and the sentencing options available to magistrates.

Many youth justice teams provide information to solicitors and barristers on the work of their units and the services

**FOR PARENTS &
YOUNG PEOPLE**

A Guide to Criminal Proceedings in
Solihull Youth Court

1. WHAT'S DIFFERENT ABOUT THE YOUTH COURT

Listed below are some of the reasons why the Youth Court is different from Adult Courts.

(a) The law is different for youths (young people up to the age of 18 years). The Youth Magistrates have different powers.

(b) The Magistrates are specially trained to deal with young people. They are sometimes called the 'Youth Bench' or panel.

(c) The law requires that parents attend with their child.

(d) The Court is private. This means that no members of the public are allowed in the Court. While the press can write about offences and the sentences passed, they cannot name the young person or their family.

2. SOME BASIC DOS AND DON'TS ON THE DAY

DO

(a) Come with your parents. (The court can demand their attendance.)

(b) Plan your journey with plenty of time to arrive at least 15 minutes before court starts.

(c) Book in at the Enquiries Desk and with the Court Usher so that the Magistrates know that you're there.

(d) Make an effort to look smart.

(e) Get help from a Solicitor. If you haven't got one already ask at the Enquiries Desk for the Duty Solicitor.

(f) Refer to the Magistrates as 'Sir' or 'Madam' when you speak to them.

(g) Ask to see the Court Officer if you want help.

DON'T

(a) Give the impression of being arrogant, like chewing gum, standing with your hands in your pockets or being generally awkward when you're in Court.

(b) Sit in to watch other Court hearings while waiting for yours; you may be called in and not hear.

(c) Cause a nuisance whilst in or around the Court building.

(d) Leave the Court building until you are told you can.

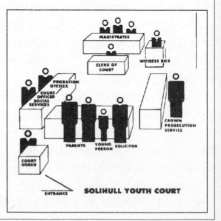

SOLIHULL YOUTH COURT

available. Some provide briefing sheets on particular cases – especially if a custodial sentence is likely to be considered. These provide counsel with the name of the person from the service in court, details of the available non-custodial options, an outline of the pre-sentence report, mitigating circumstances and general background to the offence. Some even include an outline of relevant case law and details of appeals against the use of particular sentences.

Many teams also provide information for circuit judges who will often be unfamiliar with local resources and may see very few young defendants.

Specialist projects (for example, the Edge Project in Leeds) provide judges with follow-up information on young people who have been sentenced. This allows an overview of both the young person's progress and the work of the Project. Some hold open evenings for members of the judiciary to allow discussion of these issues.

Preparation for court hearings
Pre-trial visits: The Himmat Project, Halifax

The Himmat Project, Anchor Works,
Gerrard Street, off Gibbett Street, Halifax HX1 5DG
Telephone: Halifax (0422) 348045

Many youth justice workers consider a pre-trial visit to the court a useful way of preparing a young defendant for the hearing. This is particularly the case with Crown Court hearings where the surroundings and procedures can be alien and intimidating. The visit provides an opportunity to explain the functions of different individuals and can be useful for a defendant's family.

The Himmat Project, run by the West Yorkshire Probation Service, has found this particularly useful for the Asian community. Hitherto family members often understood little of what was said in court and young people, ashamed of what their family would think, were often untruthful about the result.

A member of the Project attends each Youth or Crown Court

hearing involving an Asian defendant to provide them with support and information. The Project is described more fully in Chapter six, but its workers see this pre-court assistance as a vital part of making the court process less alienating for the defendant.

Support in court

Most youth justice teams prioritise accompanying young people to court, especially if a court report has been prepared and the offences are serious. Many services find it useful to send two officers to court. This allows the court duty officer to play a more active role in the court process, while the accompanying officer is responsible for ensuring the young person understands what is expected and for reassuring the family. It is also helpful if the accompanying officer has prepared the pre-sentence report and can give evidence or provide additional information to the court. This is particularly useful if supervision orders with specified activities are being considered.

Most of the projects or teams visited commented on the usefulness of 'Court Liaison Groups' or 'Court User Groups'. Often, these provide youth justice officers, social workers and probation officers with their only opportunity to exchange views with magistrates and respond to concerns they raise.

However, youth justice staff in some areas commented on how isolated they feel from court officials and expressed regret that previous positive contact with magistrates and court clerks was not maintained.

There appears to be a particular problem in the north-west of the country where, according to a recent report *Awaiting Trial* (Association of Chief Officers of Probation/NACRO, 1992), there is a 'culture of custody' in areas such as Bolton and Bradford, a feature of which is poor inter-agency liaison.

Chapter 4

Using the Bail Act

The quality and availability of bail support and information schemes varies across the country. Excellent bail information schemes operate in some areas but the high rates of custodial remands in others suggests that quality information is not always getting through to the defendants or the courts. This chapter looks at the ways in which both the statutory and voluntary sectors can affect bail decisions.

The Bail Act 1976

The Bail Act 1976 provides a statutory 'right' to bail unless the Court is satisfied that there are substantial grounds for believing that the defendant, if released on bail would –

a) fail to surrender to custody, or
b) commit an offence while on bail, or
c) interfere with witnesses or otherwise obstruct the course of justice.

Bail need not be granted if the court is satisfied an accused should be kept in custody for their own protection.

In granting bail the court has the following options:

o unconditional bail
o bail with conditions (no support)
o bail with conditions (with support)
o bail with conditions (accommodation and support).

The option of remand into institutional care, is discussed in the next chapter.

Bail information schemes

Bail information schemes provide the Crown Prosecution Service with verified background information on people detained overnight in police custody. The objective is to aid the

47

CPS make its recommendation to the court for bail or custodial remand.

The information is given to the CPS, the defence solicitor and the defendant.

Approved bail information schemes are overseen by two national committees whose memberships include senior personnel from the Home Office, the Probation Service, the Crown Prosecution Service and the police.

The current schemes owe their existence to a series of pilot schemes established by the Probation Services in 1986. The operation and impact of these schemes is fully discussed in Christopher Stone, *Bail Information for the Crown Prosecution Service*, 1988, and David Godson and Christopher Mitchell, *Bail Information Schemes in English Magistrates' Courts*, 1991.

Court schemes provide information for either a defendant's first appearance or a second appearance following an initial period on remand. Prison-based schemes may also provide information for the second appearance.

In May 1991, the Association of Chief Probation Officers produced a statement of principles and good practice for bail information schemes. Its key elements are:

o the presumption of liberty enshrined in the Bail Act 1976 is fundamental to the operation of a bail information scheme;
o the purpose is to promote the proper use of bail within court without resorting to the development of a surveillance role for the Probation Service and the excessive use of bail conditions; and
o bail information schemes should adopt a proactive, integral role within the daily life of the court.

East Sussex Probation Service

12 Old Steine, Brighton BN1 1EJ
Telephone: Brighton (0273) 695327

In April 1990, a bail information scheme was established at Brighton Magistrates' Court to divert appropriate defendants from a remand into custody. The scheme is notable for its success and the way in which it has been closely monitored.

It was established with the support of local magistrates and receives regular feedback from the Probation Liaison Committee.

How the scheme works
It is overseen by a local advisory group consisting of representatives from Sussex Police, the Crown Prosecution Service, the Law Society, the Justices' Clerks and the Probation Service. The Branch Crown Prosecutor has chaired the scheme since its second year of operation.

The primary duty of the scheme is to provide information to the Crown Prosecution Service and the defence solicitor which can be of assistance during a bail hearing.

East Sussex Probation Service provides a probation officer and probation assistant who interview defendants held overnight in police custody. The interview cannot take place without the defendant's consent and the information collected must be verified. This information includes material on the defendant's character, reliability, links with the local community, accommodation and employment. There is no discussion of the alleged offence. This is matter for the defendant and his/her legal representative.

When verifying the information, the probation service may contact a range of individuals and agencies, including local authority housing departments, housing associations, hostels, landlords, probation officers and social workers, the Department of Social Security, drug and alcohol treatment units, psychiatric units and general practitioners. Contact can be by telephone or in person.

The provision of such information assists the Crown Prosecution Service to form an independent view of the defendant's suitability for bail. The defence solicitor may also present the information to the court should the Crown Prosecution Service choose not to do so. The magistrate does not receive a copy of the information sheet.

The scheme is especially useful for dealing with defendants who have mental health problems. On a number of occasions, it has liaised with Health Service professionals to have prosecutions discontinued in accordance with the Crown Prosecution Service's Code of Practice.

CROWN PROSECUTION SERVICE
BAIL INFORMATION SHEET

Defendant: *Carl —*

Offence: *Burglary (Domestic)*

Next Appearance: ❏ First Appearance   ❏ Remand

   ❏ Committal   ❏ Other

Court : *— Magistrates' Court*   Date: *20 October 1993*

The Following Factors Stand in Favour of Bail:
  1. *Stable address available*
  2. *Hostel placement available*
  3. *Appropriate services available*
  4. *Community ties*

Explanation:
  1. *Mr & Mrs —, have spoken to me in person and explained that they are willing for their son Carl to return home if permitted to do so by the court.*
  2. *I have contacted, Mr —, Warden of — Bail Hostel, who confirms that a place could be made immediately available for Mr — as a bail condition. The hostel operates a minimum curfew of 11 pm to 8 am but the hostel staff would be willing to supervise an extended curfew if necessary.*
  3. *Ms J. —, Community Worker with the —, has confirmed that she is able to offer an appointment for Mr — at the Community Team Office, —, at 2 pm tomorrow 21/10/93.*
  4. *The defendant's parents have confirmed they are willing to have daily contact with their son during the bail period and 'assist him in any way possible'.*

Bail Officer: _____ Date: _____

This information has been collected by the Probation Service through an interview with the defendant and through other enquiries with the prior consent of the defendant. It is provided to both the Crown Prosecution Service and the Defence. If any further explanation is desired the officer will be available in court or can be reached at _____

Results

The scheme presently targets defendants detained in Brighton Police Station while awaiting their first appearance in Brighton Magistrates' Court. It aims to have the information available before the Court starts at 10am. If this is not possible, the probation officer will give preference to those who are more likely to be refused bail. Chief Officers of Probation recommend this preference should go to women and black defendants who, according to research (Hood,1992), are more likely to have their right to bail refused.

During 1991–92, the scheme interviewed 85% of those detained. The scheme has enjoyed good co-operation with the Sussex Police, particularly the Central Process Unit at Brighton Police Station. This has minimised burdening the custody area with requests for information.

Profiles of young defendants appearing at Brighton Magistrates' Court and interviewed under the bail information scheme over 1991–2	
Age:	half were between 17 and 25
Gender:	93% were male
Ethnic Origin:	93% were white
Accommodation:	Most were local to the Brighton area and living in non-permanent accommodation. 20% were of no fixed abode.*
Employment:	78% were unemployed, an increase of 11% on the previous year's figures, in an area where the average was 11%. The number in training or education was only 2%.
Social Problems:	69% had clearly definable problems with drugs or alcohol, mental health and emotional problems or welfare related difficulties.**

* Figures provided with the co-operation of community groups including the YMCA and bed and breakfast establishments.

** The scheme has maintained a high level of contact with the local statutory and voluntary services assisting those with drug and alcohol problems in order to maximise the chances of securing bail.

Bail support schemes

Bail support schemes are designed to offer an alternative to custodial remand in either a prison or secure accommodation. They are based on the principle that removal from home can be disruptive, can reinforce a defendant's self-perception of criminality and can lead to a greater risk of re-offending. Bail support packages must address the issues which have a direct bearing on the possibility of custody.

It is usually preferable to provide packages which can support a defendant within his/her own community. Such support can focus upon measures that offer stability and reduce the risk of re-offending such as permanent and safe accommodation, employment and constructive use of leisure time.

Careful consideration should also be given to the nature of the offence, any offending pattern and any danger to the public.

Bail support packages often have conditions attached such as curfews or non-association orders. It is the responsibility of the police to monitor these conditions, not those offering bail support.

Surrey Bail Support Scheme

Surrey Youth Justice Team, Sheratts House, Mayford Green, Woking, Surrey GU22 0PP
Telephone: Woking (0483) 723922

Background

This scheme started in January 1991 in response to growing concern over the large number of young people in Surrey being remanded into care, secure accommodation or custody.

The scheme is the product of a partnership between the Royal Philanthropic Society and Surrey Social Services. The project co-ordinator is employed by the Royal Philanthropic Society and seconded to the Surrey Youth Justice Service, an inter-agency service managed jointly by Surrey Probation Service and Social Services.

The scheme aims to assist young people under 18 to secure bail by providing community-based support and supplies information and advice regarding bail and remand issues to the courts, court officers and the young people themselves.

How it works
The Bail Support Co-ordinator liaises with the court duty officers in the 11 scheduled courts in Surrey. If possible, other courts are covered when a young person is being refused bail. There is good liaison with bail information officers regarding 17 year olds detained in police custody and with the out-of-hours social work teams regarding special court sittings.

Bail support work focuses upon bringing stability into a young person's life. Additional support includes:

○ support to a family to enable the young person to return home;
○ accommodation, in collaboration with the Surrey Accommodation Scheme, for those who are unable to return home:
○ liaison with the Education Department to address problems of attendance or exclusion and to ensure educational needs are met; and
○ contact with sessional workers, both during the week and at weekends, to plan a more constructive use of leisure time.

The co-ordinator interviews the young person, either at home or in the custodial institution, and prepares information for the court. Every effort is made to ensure comprehensive information goes before the court. Family and friends may be interviewed and there is close contact with Youth Justice Team members and the author of any pre-sentence report.

It is now very rare for juveniles to be refused bail in Surrey.

Bail Out Support Scheme (BOSS) Southend

BOSS, 17 Weston Road, Southend-on-Sea, Essex SS1 1AS
Telephone: Southend-on-Sea (0702) 330464.

Background
Remands into the care of the Local Authority often inappropriately use the precious and diminishing residential resources of Social Services and put great strain on the existing services they have to

offer their clients. They are unable to offer any great levels of supervision for the young person, therefore they are unable to respond adequately to the immediate needs of the young person.

(BOSS Report, January–December 1988)

This scheme was established in January 1988 after negotiations between Essex County Council and the Rainer Foundation. Its aims are:

o to offer a community-based alternative to remands into care or custody;
o to provide a facility for those young people for whom conventional bail conditions have failed;
o to minimise the disruption of the young person's positive community links such as family, education and employment during the remand period; and
o to provide a more cost-effective service to the courts.

The scheme places particular emphasis on supporting young people in their own home environment and equipping them with the necessary skills to resist re-offending.

Its particular concerns with remands into care are:

o they provide no real sanctions to control young people;
o there is little commitment by the young people because of the short-term nature of the placement (on average, less than 4 weeks);
o older residents influence younger ones in the same way as in custodial institutions;
o there can be further offending by groups on remand in the same residential home;
o there is interference with school and employment if placed out of Southend;
o specialist provision is expensive.

How the scheme works
a) Referrals
The agency or solicitor concerned notifies the scheme. The Bail Support Worker liaises with the parent(s), Social Services and

Who is BOSS for?

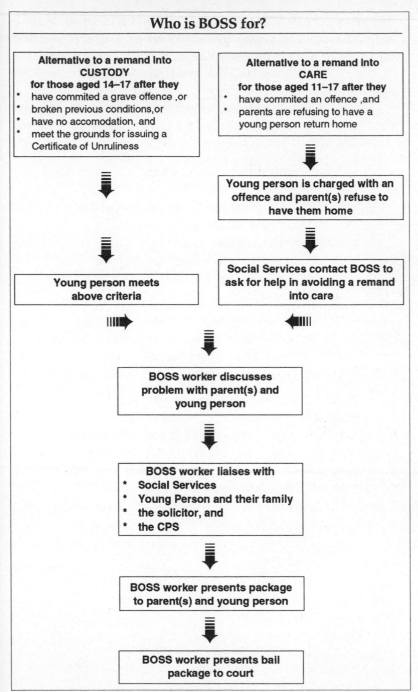

Alternative to a remand into CUSTODY
for those aged 14–17 after they
* have commited a grave offence ,or
* broken previous conditions,or
* have no accomodation, and
* meet the grounds for issuing a
  Certificate of Unruliness

Alternative to a remand into CARE
for those aged 11–17 after they
* have commited an offence ,and
* parents are refusing to have a
  young person return home

Young person is charged with an offence and parent(s) refuse to have them home

Young person meets above criteria

Social Services contact BOSS to ask for help in avoiding a remand into care

BOSS worker discusses problem with parent(s) and young person

BOSS worker liaises with
* Social Services
* Young Person and their family
* the solicitor, and
* the CPS

BOSS worker presents package to parent(s) and young person

BOSS worker presents bail package to court

the defence solicitor and decides whether bail support is appropriate. The solicitor first makes an application for unconditional bail. If this is unacceptable, a BOSS package is offered. There are difficulties with this procedure if there is insufficient advance notice. At times, the lack of a regular court officer from Southend Social Services has also reduced effective communication.

Having settled into a placement, the young person embarks on an assessment period comprising the following elements:

○ offending behaviour and decision making;
○ a review of the young person's values;
○ self-image
○ improving social skills; and
○ better self-control.

Following this assessment, the young person and the staff member agree on ways to address problems arising from one or more of the above areas. Other concerns the programme may also address include family relationships, education and employment problems, DSS problems and improving liaison between solicitors, the CPS, Social Services, Probation and the police.

b)   Liaison with the solicitor
There are difficulties unless the solicitor regularly deals with juvenile clients, particularly in relation to Sections 60 and 62 of the 1991 Criminal Justice Act (replacing Certificates of Unruliness). BOSS scheme workers have to ensure they provide the solicitor with accurate information about both the law and the scheme.

c)   Accommodation
The scheme has established supported lodgings for those young people for whom removal from the home is a positive or necessary step. Frequent changes to DSS regulations and delays with payment have made bed and breakfast landlords reluctant to take on young people. A clear agreement between Social Services and the DSS is necessary.

d) *Programmes*

There is an emphasis on individual packages for each young person referred to the scheme. In the majority of cases, magistrates have granted bail with a residence condition and a requirement to comply with the BOSS scheme.

Case Study 1: Rita, aged 16
Offence: robbery
Previous: none

BOSS involvement began following a request from the police for an appropriate adult at a PACE interview.

Rita had masqueraded as a 20 year old for several months. At the time of the robbery, she had used this identity and had been remanded to a bail hostel as an adult. She re-offended whilst on bail and had absconded from the hostel. She was now at a high risk of being remanded into custody and admitted her true identity and age to her solicitor.

BOSS attended the PACE interview to assess whether Rita was at risk of remand to local authority accommodation. Rita disclosed that she had absconded from secure accommodation in Glasgow nine months ago. She had lived and 'worked the streets' in London, eventually settling and working in Southend. The offence of robbery occurred when Rita persuaded a man to return to her accommodation for sex. A male associate was waiting for them to return and then held a knife to this man's throat and demanded money.

The Magistrates' Court agreed to BOSS involvement as part of Rita's bail conditions. This successfully prevented a remand into local authority care which would have meant her returning to court every week (potentially from Scotland.)

BOSS had two main functions during Rita's time before sentencing. The first was to support and advise Rita whilst on bail. The second was to act as a mediator between the Scottish local authority and Rita. This arose because there was a warrant out for Rita's arrest for absconding from the Secure Unit in Glasgow. After the failure of initial negotiations, Rita was arrested by two Scottish officers, taken in hand-cuffs by train to Glasgow and held there overnight. She had now spent three nights in police custody.

Within two weeks, Rita had returned to Southend, her Secure Accommodation Order discharged but with her Supervision Order in place.

Rita consistently attended the scheme and made good use of the support on offer. She often spoke of her experiences of self-injury, disruptive behaviour and substance abuse whilst in care. She disclosed details of sexual and physical abuse by her stepfather and by a worker whilst in care. She admitted that the pattern of her behaviour was a product of these experiences and that she often became involved in relationships with men she perceived as powerful. She 'worked the street' to maintain her passion for expensive clothes which made her feel 'special'. She viewed the punters as weak, insignificant and inadequate which made her feel powerful and in control.

BOSS had regular contact with Rita's social worker in Scotland. This was time-consuming but ensured Rita's welfare needs were met. Rita returned to Scotland over the Christmas period to enable reports to be written for Crown Court. She stayed at a children's home and continued to work the streets.

After returning to Southend, Rita found her accommodation was no longer available. BOSS liaised with the Scottish and local Social Services to secure payment for her to stay in a small hotel until more permanent accommodation could be found in the Southend area.

BOSS accompanied Rita to the Crown Court for her sentence for the robbery and spoke on her behalf regarding the work that had been done over the previous seventeen weeks. Rita's positive response to BOSS convinced the court that a community-based disposal was appropriate and she was given a one-year supervision order with intensive treatment.

Rita has now settled in Southend and her Scottish supervision order has been discharged.

Case Study 2: Peter, aged 17
Offence: TWOC x 3, theft x 2 and ABH
Previous: 53 offences and 36 TICs, mainly domestic burglary, theft and one robbery

Peter was arrested for taking and driving away without consent and also charged with kicking a police officer whilst trying to escape. BOSS was called to court by Social Services because the police were applying for a custodial remand.

The assessment of Peter's suitability took place in the court cells. Peter said he had taken the drug Tamazipan, together with alcohol, and could not remember taking a car nor assaulting a female officer.

Peter had been successfully placed on BOSS on three occasions over the last four years. BOSS was confident he would attend the scheme but doubted the likely extent of his co-operation. Since last being on the scheme, Peter had served two YOI sentences and had received a 12-hour Attendance Centre Order for re-offending. He now faced six further charges. There was clearly a lot of work to be done!

BOSS presented a package to the court consisting of daily contact for the first two weeks followed by regular sessions. The aim was to provide supervision, support and help with issues of self-control. Peter would be set clear boundaries and goals, with the main expectation being he would attend regularly and punctually. He would be referred for assistance with his drug abuse and given help in seeking suitable employment.

The Youth Court accepted the proposal and imposed a curfew and residence conditions with his parents.

Three workers saw Peter during his remand period. They worked primarily on his employment situation, visiting the DSS, Job Centre, Careers Service and training schemes. Peter was initially unenthusiastic but took an interest in a construction training course. He was also paid a bridging allowance while awaiting interviews. This was the first official payment he had ever received.

Peter was unable to get a referral to the local drugs unit so BOSS attempted to do some work around the problem. Peter's awareness of the dangers of certain drugs was low and he admitted to mixing drugs and alcohol regularly. It appeared his drug taking was less an addiction than a means by which he could avoid responsibility for his actions. His alcohol consumption had risen dramatically since leaving custody and his parents said he was much more prone to mood swings and flying into a temper.

Peter's family was very supportive during BOSS's involvement and continued to encourage him away from the persistent and opportunistic offending in which he engaged.

Seven weeks into the remand, a BOSS worker saw Peter drinking in a pub during his curfew period. With some reluctance, BOSS notified the police to ensure the scheme's credibility and to make it clear to Peter that there would be no collusion with him. BOSS also told Peter what they had done but made it clear they remained committed to working with him. This remained possible when the police surprisingly chose not to follow up the breach.

Peter was offered an interview for an electronics training course to take place two weeks after his sentence. This gave Peter a clear focus away from a further custodial sentence. This, combined with his regular attendance and commitment to the scheme, contributed to his receiving a one-year probation order.

Results

During the first year of the scheme, there were 15 young people on bail support for a total of 107 weeks; 9 eventually received a non-custodial sentence.

The cost of one week of bail support was £55 compared to £300 per week in a children's home, £400 per week in a prison and £1,000 per week in a secure unit.

A comparison of those on the scheme in 1988 and 1990 shows:

o the alleged offences were much more serious in 1990, indicating that young people who would in the past have gone to custodial remand were being sent instead to BOSS;

o 58% were given a direct alternative to custody in 1990 compared with 33% in 1988;

o 52% offended while on BOSS in 1990 compared with 66% in 1988. Those who did were usually given another chance;

o in 1990, 17 young people spent a total of 178 weeks on bail at an average of 10.4 weeks each compared with 15 young people for a total of 109 weeks at an average of 7.2 weeks. This was despite court proceedings dropping by 22%.

Future developments

During 1992, proposals were drawn up to extend the scheme throughout Essex using the Home Office Grants Scheme. However, these have failed to materialise and it now appears that local Youth Justice Centres will make their own arrangements.

Stonehouse Probation Hostel

125 Harleston Road, Northampton NN5 6AA
Telephone: Northampton (0604) 752112

Background

The Stonehouse Project is the product of a partnership between the Rainer Foundation and the Northamptonshire Probation Service. It aims to:

o provide a community-based resource to which the court may either sentence or remand young adults aged between 17 and 22.

- provide individualised programmes for young adults which will divert them from a pattern of offending and provide them with new opportunities and skills;
- work in partnership with the Northamptonshire Probation Service and all other agencies within the criminal justice system; and
- ensure that services are provided regardless of race and to look at ways the service can be developed to meet the needs of young women.

The Project has three major client groups – those who are remanded on bail with a condition of residence at the hostel, those who are on a bail support programme with a condition of residence and those who are directed to live at the hostel as a condition of their probation order.

The main building is a large house close to the centre of Northampton which provides accommodation for a maximum of 16 residents. Three houses are rented nearby for use as additional units for those requiring less supervision. Women are also placed in these houses because it is thought inappropriate to place them in the main building.

How it works

The Stonehouse staff regard the following circumstances as common to most of the young people who use the Project:

- a low self-image;
- a chaotic lifestyle, many having been in local authority care;
- an inability to cope with authority;
- a lack of self-control, including anger control, and fluctuating behaviour patterns;
- an inability to resist peer-group pressure;
- damaged and/or broken family relationships;
- a high incidence of unemployment; and
- alcohol, solvent and soft drug abuse.

Services at the scheme are therefore designed to address such problems and to ensure that it is not, as one staff member put it, 'a glorified baby-sitting service'.

The services offered by the hostel include:

Programmes

Hostel Residence	Bail Support
Work programmes	Minimum of 3 visits per week
Employment training	Programmes for
Social skills	individual needs
	24-hour crisis intervention
Education	
Counselling	
Relationship resolution	
Accommodation resolution	
Work to reduce offending	
Conditions	
To reside at Stonehouse	To reside at Stonehouse or as directed by staff
To abide by the rules	To comply with bail support programme

The Bail Hostel

An important feature of the hostel is that it is open 24 hours a day, 365 days a year. This means young adults, including those who have left the project, have access to services at any time. It enables individual and group programmes to be run outside of normal office hours. It means a crisis can be dealt with immediately and not when it is administratively convenient. This flexibility, combined with the level of supervision and the commitment of the staff, has given local judges and magistrates confidence in the scheme.

Support and advice

The Project places a great emphasis on providing support and advice services. This involves working with community agencies such as drug and alcohol advice groups and developing a wide network of agencies which can offer support to young people. As a result, the young people get to know more about the local services and particularly useful links have been made with employment agencies and vocational training groups.

Bail support project

In April 1991, a pilot bail support scheme was established in the hostel following an injection of funds from the Home Office and the Pilgrim Trust.

The scheme's programmes offer support and declining levels of supervision depending on whether the young person is based at the hostel, the cluster houses or in the community.

When establishing the project, care was take to avoid the courts imposing a bail support programme on a defendant who would otherwise have been granted bail with few or no conditions.

It was therefore agreed that the Probation Service would continue to provide its normal bail information service while the new scheme would cater for 17- to 21-year-old defendants who have already been remanded into custody and consequently require a change of circumstance before being granted bail.

The probation liaison officer refers suitable clients. The defendant is interviewed in custody and the family is visited at home.

If appropriate, a bail support package is offered at the next court appearance. Each programme includes a detailed plan of accommodation, employment/training, leisure activities, specialist help (if required) and details of the proposed level of supervision.

The court is requested to impose a condition that the young person either resides at the hostel, in the smaller attached houses or as directed by the bail support staff.

An important element of the scheme is the close liaison maintained with the police who are informed of any breaches of bail or further offending. This may lead to a further bail application requesting the defendant be moved into the more closely supervised surroundings of the bail hostel.

At the end of the bail period, the bail support worker submits a separate report to the Court and also provides information for the pre-sentence report.

Dover Bail Hostel

Dover Bail Hostel, 13 Park Avenue, Dover Kent CT16 1ES
Telephone: Dover (0304) 242748

Background
This hostel opened in early 1990 and provides 15 beds for referrals from Magistrates' Courts in Kent.

Those referred are, by definition, homeless, but all are encouraged and assisted to seek more permanent 'move-on' accommodation before their final court appearance.

How it works
Residents are accepted after a telephone referral, with a decision usually being made within an hour. All referrals must be made via a probation officer. There is no assessment period but the hostel staff are happy to discuss potential referrals with the police, the CPS and defence solicitors.

Bail hostels do not provide the same level of supervision or intervention as the schemes discussed either earlier in this chapter or in the following chapter. However, they do ensure that someone is not placed in custody simply for being homeless.

What are the rules?
The Conditions of Residence cover the residents' obligation to:

o abide by the overnight curfew;
o pay the weekly rent;
o behave well – refrain from violent and disruptive behaviour, and not bring alcohol or drugs into the hostel;
o have a medical examination after arrival.

Residents who fail to keep these rules are taken back to court for breach of bail proceedings and are not allowed to return to the hostel.

Residents are expected to abide by the Hostel's rules but are otherwise responsible for themselves. There is a weekly hostel meeting and each resident is assigned a key-worker, usually an assistant warden, to take a special interest in his or her progress, to ensure good liaison with the home probation officer, to provide counselling and advice and to assist in seeking a move-on address.

Results

Of the 147 residents who passed through the hostel in 1991/92, 90% received a non-custodial sentence. Only nine residents were returned to court for failure to abide by hostel rules.

At present, about 70% of residents remain successfully at the hostel until a court date or relocation to an alternative bail address.

Case Study 1: Alice, aged 22

Alice stayed in the hostel for 259 days during 1992. She had been charged with armed robbery which was reduced to conspiracy to rob. She and her two co-defendants (one of whom was her husband) were initially remanded into custody.

After Alice was bailed, her 2-year-old child was fostered locally so contact could be maintained. Alice was also able to get help in finding local, permanent accommodation.

Alice was eventually given a probation order for her role in the offence. Her co-defendants received long prison sentences. Social Services returned Alice's child and Alice gave birth to a second child shortly after sentence. She has not re-offended to date.

Case Study 2: Jaspal

Jaspal stayed in the hostel for 126 days during 1991–1992. He had been charged with possession of a canister of noxious liquid and was initially remanded into custody.

Being bailed to the hostel meant he could leave the negative influences of his home area and develop his social skills. He decided to remain in the local area and acquired a job and accommodation.

Jaspal pleaded not guilty to the charge but was convicted and sentenced to 28 days imprisonment with £200 costs. He was released immediately because of the time he had spent on remand.

He is still in the same employment and has been promoted. He has not re-offended.

Case Study 3: Ruth, aged 19

Ruth stayed at the hostel for 104 days during 1991. She faced charges of theft and deception, had absconded from previous hostels and had served 3 custodial sentences. Staff at the hostel said she gave them a lot of 'headaches'.

However, the patience of the staff and the stable environment allowed Ruth to learn to trust people and to reduce her solvent and drug abuse.

Ruth was pregnant when she was referred and was encouraged to sustain ante-natal care. The hostel liaised with her home area to obtain accommodation.

She was given a probation order which was successfully completed in July 1992. She has moved to a mother and baby hostel and has a better relationship with her family. She has not re-offended.

Chapter 5

Avoiding Prison Remands

Philip Knight started to play truant from school and to steal when he was 13. His parents were advised to have him placed in care. He kept running away and, trying to get home, he grabbed a handbag from a café table. The bag contained £1,600 and he had inadvertently committed a serious offence. He was granted bail and sent back to a children's home. There, he slashed his wrists. He was moved and his behaviour deteriorated. Social workers applied for a Certificate of Unruliness, which effectively sent him to prison. Within days, he had slashed his wrists again. He was placed in a strip cell for two nights. In July 1990, Philip was found dead in Swansea Prison. He was just 15 years of age.

Howard League, 1992

It is clear that the whole criminal justice system failed Philip. His story begs the question: what else could have been done to help him? This chapter identifies a number of projects which have provided courts with imaginative alternatives to penal custody and have had an impact on the numbers remanded into custody.

Policy Considerations

In February 1991, the Home Office produced the consultative paper *The Remand of Alleged Juvenile Offenders* which stated:

> Remanding juveniles in Prison Department custody is not a step that should be taken lightly . . . Custodial remands should be seen as a last resort and used only where there is a need to protect the public from serious harm or the alleged repeated offending.

The Criminal Justice Act 1991 came into force on 1 October 1992. It made it illegal to place 14 year olds in custody but kept the option for 15- and 16-year-old boys when 'the court is of the opinion that only remanding him to a remand centre or prison would be adequate to protect the public from serious harm'.

Under the Act, remands for 15 and 16 year olds were due to be phased out over the next four years. The Department of Health subsequently announced it would fund the provision of 60–65 additional beds in secure accommodation under local authority control. However, local authorities are expected to pay for the running costs of the new secure units and many are reluctant to take up the additional responsibilities on the Department's terms.

As part of the proposed shift to local secure care for 15- and 16-year-old remand prisoners, the Criminal Justice Act 1991 gave courts the power to:

o impose conditions of the kind that can be imposed when granting bail;
o stipulate that a juvenile must not be placed by the local authority with a named person; and
o require that a 15 or 16 year old be held in secure accommodation (the security requirement).

The security requirement does not become operational until the new facilities become available. It will also apply to 15- and 16-year-old girls who presently cannot be remanded into custody. It does not apply to 17 year olds who, for bail purposes, are treated the same as adults even though they are juveniles under the Act.

Since the commencement of the Act, much of the discussion concerning changing remand arrangements has been clouded by the separate issue of sentencing options for 12–15 year olds. The Howard League has dealt with the Home Secretary's proposals elsewhere (*Young and in Trouble*, 1993). The experience of the 1980s suggests that significant inroads can be made into the prison remand population by schemes similar to these which have played a part in reducing the use of custodial sentences over the past ten years.

Start Point, South Devon Social Services and the Children's Society

Start Point, 42 Palace Avenue, Paignton, Devon TQ3 3HF
Telephone: Paignton (0803) 666055

Background

Grouping troubled and troublesome teenagers together increased the likelihood of long stays in care and custody. It was depressing work, staff were under extreme pressure. The future for children has, in these establishments, been extremely bleak, and they knew it. Petty crime was commonplace. Project leader, Nigel Hinks, 1990

The very essence of 'Start Point' requires a commitment to the eradication of conditions that result in long periods of group living. The work undertaken by the short-stay accommodation service incorporates planned respite and shared care for up to forty days, a crisis/emergency provision and a remand place when alternatives to care have been ruled out. Our objective is the restoration of young people to their families or alternative care placements within an agreed social work plan. Start Point Information Sheet

In 1987, the Children's Society and South Devon Social Services commissioned research from Bath University to examine the circumstances of young people remanded into care. The Children's Society's involvement in this area dates back to the establishment of St Faiths Children's Home in 1918. Their experience was that children come into care in an unplanned way at times of crisis. This especially applied to children placed in care on remand.

The University study confirmed this and highlighted how the availability of institutional care meant other options for young people in trouble were not being pursued. Put bluntly, if the beds were there, they would be used and community-based schemes such as remand fostering would not be developed.

In 1988, as a result of the Bath University study, the Children's Society prepared a successful submission to the Social Services Department arguing that teenagers with problematic behaviour were being repeatedly failed by social work and that residential care was inappropriate for this client group.

The Children's Society proposed a new project offering a range of services not dependent on residential care. Priority would be given to working with young people and their families in their own homes and working in a more proactive manner when care services were requested.

How it works

In 1990, the St Faiths building was sold and replaced by a small, ordinary house nearby. This was a conscious attempt to move away from an identifiable children's-home setting.

Re-named Start Point and known simply as 497, this new project deals with young people who are unable immediately to return home. The project provides eight short-stay beds, one of which is available for a young person on remand. Other beds may be available for a young person who requires accommodation as part of a bail support package.

The Start Point team has prioritised remands to custody and care as the starting point of its work. The provision of accommodation is limited to a maximum stay of 8 days with the focus on securing an alternative, and more appropriate, community placement.

A social worker liaises with Start Point over each case in which remand to local authority accommodation is possible.

The Start Point staff then works through the available options including:

○ providing information in court to assist with bail;
○ providing a bail address, either with family or friends;
○ independent accommodation or accommodation within Start Point;
○ providing supervision during bail;
○ providing supervision for a young person on remand living at home; and
○ providing accommodation at Start Point while the young person is remanded.

At court, individual plans are presented by the Start Point staff which often reflect the creative thinking of the project. Proposals can include the youngster being returned to his/her family with a member of the Start Point staff visiting on a contractual basis to help deal with difficult family relationships, problems of control within the home or drug or alcohol abuse. Special care is given to following up each remand case. After each remand, the case is reviewed by the Start Point staff, giving another opportunity to ensure the family, the young person and the support workers understand what is required of them.

It also provides another opportunity to establish a supportive relationship with the young person while making it clear that changes to the young person's lifestyle will be required.

Case Study: John, aged 17

John's case illustrates the negative effects of the group living and custody which can characterise a young person's career path through the criminal justice system.

Between October 1989 and April 1990, John was remanded into care and placed at Start Point on three occasions. The project was still based at the old-style, institutional setting of St Faiths and John absconded frequently, committed more serious offences and used unknown quantities and types of drugs. During the same period, he also spent 3 months in a YOI, was remanded into care and placed in secure accommodation. Clearly, repeated residential stays were exacerbating, not resolving, John's difficulties.

Start Point therefore worked with John in a different way between July and December 1991. For a short period, John and a Start Point worker moved to accommodation in a remote location. This broke the pattern of his behaviour and, on his return, John moved to independent accommodation where he received support from another agency.

Start Point worked with John between March and April 1992 after he had again been remanded into care. By now, the project was based at 497 where the accommodation service was quite different from that offered at St Faith's.

His stay at 497 was positive and beneficial to his health. There were few signs of the behaviour he exhibited at St Faith's and the team feels this confirms the effectiveness of the new service.

Results

This has been one of the most successful schemes of its kind. The length of stay in the remand bed has been less than three days in 70 per cent of cases. The bed has not been used at all since April 1992.

There have been many referrals to the remand bed which the court has allowed to be diverted to bail and support from the project once an alternate package has been proposed.

The following table illustrates the changing nature of the service which Start Point provides:

Service provided	Apr 89– Mar 90	Apr 90– Mar 91	Apr 91– Mar 92	Apr 92– Mar 93
Accommodation only	8 (100%)	3 (50%)	0 (50%)	0 (20%)
Accommodation and service	3	8	17	2
Bail information	2	9	13	20
Bail supervision	0	8	7	1
Remand supervision	1	2	2	1
PACE	0	0	12	3
Total	**11**	**22**	**34**	**25**

The sale of St Faiths has enabled Start Point to develop a range of additional services aimed at keeping young people out of institutional care. These include an accommodation service, a preparation for independent living scheme, an advice and counselling service and a youth crime service. The scope of these services is illustrated by the following case study:

Case Study: Ben, aged 15

Ben was staying out at night and stealing and his parents were completely fed up with him. Social Services were involved and Start Point staff argued against him being removed and placed into local authority care. Ben stayed at home whilst also coming to 497 as part of a short-term plan.

Things improved until he was caught supplying drugs to fellow school pupils. Police also discovered Ben was fraudulently passing his father's cheques and credit cards. This time, Ben's mother decided she had had enough and pleaded that he be taken into care. With Ben suspended from school and likely to be expelled, she felt she could no longer cope. Ben wanted to be at home and to try and return to school. Negotiations with social workers and Ben's school led to his return on a promise of good behaviour for the summer. The family breakdown was also tackled by helping Ben, his father, mother and brother look together at their problems. Each got the help they needed – counselling, family sessions, information about leisure pursuits and housing advice.

Soon Ben's behaviour and relationships at home improved. After completing his final year at school, he is now about to start work for the first time.

The encouraging results to date make the joint policy statement issued by the project's management particularly worthy of note:

> Our fundamental belief is in the ability of the community to show tolerance to resolve and heal situations rather than resort to formal processing through prosecution and the court and care systems.

South Glamorgan Remand Panel

South Glamorgan Social Services, Youth Justice, Penhill, The Rise, Penhill Road, Cardiff CF1 9PR
Telephone: Cardiff (0222) 568658

Background
South Glamorgan Social Services has adopted a different approach. It has developed a system for intervening in the remand process in order to provide information to the courts and services which averts the need for institutional care. Their practice has developed out of major changes made to the remand system in South Glamorgan during 1990 and their responsibilities and tasks are clearly set out in the Departmental Procedures.

Pre-Trial Intervention Team (PRINT)
This was established in March 1990 to target young people held in a police station or in court who are at risk of being remanded into care or custody. The team aims to provide

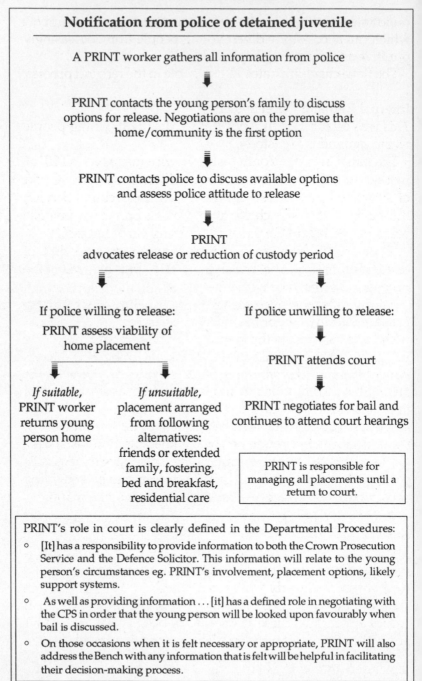

Notification from police of detained juvenile

A PRINT worker gathers all information from police

PRINT contacts the young person's family to discuss options for release. Negotiations are on the premise that home/community is the first option

PRINT contacts police to discuss available options and assess police attitude to release

PRINT advocates release or reduction of custody period

If police willing to release:
PRINT assess viability of home placement

If police unwilling to release:

PRINT attends court

If suitable, PRINT worker returns young person home

If unsuitable, placement arranged from following alternatives: friends or extended family, fostering, bed and breakfast, residential care

PRINT negotiates for bail and continues to attend court hearings

PRINT is responsible for managing all placements until a return to court.

PRINT's role in court is clearly defined in the Departmental Procedures:

o [It] has a responsibility to provide information to both the Crown Prosecution Service and the Defence Solicitor. This information will relate to the young person's circumstances eg. PRINT's involvement, placement options, likely support systems.

o As well as providing information . . . [it] has a defined role in negotiating with the CPS in order that the young person will be looked upon favourably when bail is discussed.

o On those occasions when it is felt necessary or appropriate, PRINT will also address the Bench with any information that is felt will be helpful in facilitating their decision-making process.

rapid intervention, accurate information and intensive support which can successfully divert young people from increasingly punitive and damaging experiences.

The flow-chart illustrates PRINT's role in the remand process:

Internal Remand Panel System
This was established in April 1990 to deal with young people facing remand into custody.

The panel includes Youth Justice Service managers, a PRINT worker and, if required, a probation officer. It operates as part of an agreed procedure with the Crown Prosecution Service, the police and court clerks and aims to prevent a juvenile being placed before the panel considering his or her case.

There are still some cases getting through the net – 69% of cases went before the panel in 1991 – but generally, the procedure seems to be working well.

After notification from the CPS, the panel meets at 9 am to prepare information for the morning's hearing.

The panel discusses the nature of the offence and the young person's home circumstances. It looks at mitigating factors which support the young person staying at home or in alternative accommodation and weighs them against the need to protect both the young person and the community.

Support services are designed to reflect the seriousness of the offence and the young person's vulnerable circumstances.

This system allows magistrates to decide on issues of public protection and the local authority to concentrate on providing constructive and effective alternatives to custodial remands.

Results
The cumulative effect of these changes has been a reduction in the number of young people removed from home into residential care or custody whilst on remand.

According to the South Glamorgan Social Services ' . . . it would appear that these changes have been achieved without adverse effects in terms of public protection – indeed, the fall in custody, custodial remands and the marginal fall in juvenile crime would indicate the reverse.'

The following chart illustrates the reduction:

Comparison of figures 1989–1992 for those remanded into custody

	1989/90	1990/91	1991/92
Number of episodes	35	23	8
Number of weeks	91	65	9

Some comments on the 1991/92 figures should be made. Reports offering an alternative to custody were presented for each of the eight boys on each occasion they appeared in court. The alternatives were taken up in the cases of five of the boys and they were released. However, none of the three who stayed in custody was given a custodial sentence. This begs the question of why the young people were originally remanded into custody. If the safety of the public was the paramount reason, the sentencing decisions are inconsistent.

Case Study: Terry, aged 16

Terry was charged with a section 18 wounding. He had fired an air rifle in a public place and injured a young girl. He had three previous convictions for minor, unrelated offences. When he first appeared before a Juvenile Court, he was remanded into custody despite a recommendation for remand into care. Two days later, Terry again appeared in court with a recommendation that he be remanded into care and placed with foster parents outside the immediate area. The court accepted the recommendation and Terry complied with all of his bail conditions.

A considerable time later, Terry received a six-month prison sentence. This was a disappointing decision, inconsistent with the attitudes shown pre-trial. However, it is an example of how the Remand Panel can be instrumental in diverting young people away from immediate custody.

Case Study: Alex, aged 15

Alex was charged with going equipped, interfering with and being carried in stolen vehicles. PRINT was not notified of his first appearance on 27 February 1992 and he was remanded into custody at HMP Cardiff on the grounds that he had 'persistently absconded from a community home'. He subsequently appeared on three further occasions at which proposals for supported bail were refused by the court. On his fifth appearance, on 26 March 1992, Alex was given a Supervision Order with Intermediate Treatment. Alex's case is a disturbing reminder of how vulnerable young people are still being remanded into the prison system.

After Alex's fourth appearance, the Social Services Department wrote to the Magistrates at the Vale of Glamorgan Juvenile Court expressing their concern.

The letter stated:

'Alex's four week remand in Cardiff Prison has meant him being locked up in a shared cell for 23 hours a day. A cell which he has had to share with an older young person whom Alex alleges has bullied him and threatened him. Such circumstances have certainly put Alex's health and well-being at risk, especially when the necessity of Alex being there has been questioned . . . .

'There are many young people in the juvenile justice system with similar or much worse records of offending than Alex. Many of these will at times abscond from local authority accommodation as Alex himself has done. If all these young people were to be accommodated in secure accommodation or in prison custody, the demand would far outweigh the places available at present and what has been estimated by the Welsh Office for the future . . . '

The magistrates also received a copy of a letter sent to the governor of the prison by a representative of Barnados. This letter expressed serious concern that Alex, who had been visited three times by Barnados' staff, 'had been talking about how 15 year olds commit suicide in prisons'.

In this case, Alex was released before serious harm was done. Hopefully, this book provides alternatives for responding to young people like Alex.

Kirklees Remand Fostering Scheme

Youth Justice Section, Somerset Buildings, Church Street, Huddersfield , West Yorkshire HD1 1DD
Telephone: Huddersfield (0484) 422133
(Kirklees Council number – ask for Youth Justice Section)

. . . periods on remand are often crucial for young people in terms of their eventual sentence and in terms of checking further offending during a period when young people may feel unmotivated or that

they have little to lose. The period of remand should remain a highly active one, during which the main focus is the stabilisation of behaviour and preparation for the court appearance.'

Mark Feeney, Principal Officer

Background

The Remand Fostering Project has been set up by Kirklees Social Services Department to provide an additional facility to the local authority residential accommodation in the Structured Unit at Dewsbury. Remand fostering involves placing young people with specially recruited foster parents.

In Kirklees, there are four families who are currently able to offer accommodation to one young person at a time. The foster parents are paid £80 per week. This is slightly more than the average for foster parents in the area and reflects the difficult nature of the task. A £40 retainer fee is paid whilst the families have a vacant bed. Attempts are made to reflect the diversity of the local community, including positive efforts to recruit families from within ethnic minorities.

The Youth Justice Service runs this specialist programme and trains and supports the carers. The training is an important part of the scheme. Offering a home to a young person who is awaiting trial can be a difficult and demanding task which involves risks for carers and a sensitivity to the special needs of young people. Those who offer their homes must be supportive and prepared to address some of the problems associated with offending. They must be flexible, patient and consistent in managing the expectations of the house.

A typical training programme run by the Youth Justice Service staff covers the following areas:

1. *Youth offending in context*
   Why do young people offend? The basic aims of youth justice and an introduction to the range of services in Kirklees.
2. *The Youth Court*
   What is the jurisdiction of the court? Who is present? A basic outline of the criminal justice process: arrest, police station interview, bail information, bail support and

remands to local authority accommodation and the final court appearance.

3. *Remand fostering and bail support*
   The remand process, the aims and objectives of remand fostering and the work undertaken with young people during this period.

4. *The options available to the local authority*
   A basic outline of the available services, including secure unit services.

5. *The process of remand fostering*
   A detailed look at the aims and objectives of the service, including the statutory rules and regulations. A full discussion of the purposes of placements and the possible difficulties.

6. *The Police and Criminal Evidence Act 1984*
   A discussion of the Act with special attention given to the role of the appropriate adult.

There is additional training on managing adolescent behaviour and the implications of the Children Act 1989 and Criminal Justice Act 1991.

Training is undertaken either on block days or in a series of evening sessions.

When is a remand carer used?

A substitute family is the preferable option when a young person is unable to return home. It is not appropriate if the young person is unable to survive in a family environment or the alleged offence is so serious as to put the family and young person at risk.

The use of remand carers has the following advantages:

- placement in a family can offer a more homely and sensitive environment than a residential or remand unit;
- there can be a more effective response to a young person's individual needs;
- remand carers can offer a more flexible package of care and support;
- the support offered is less intrusive than institutional care

and is often regarded as less provocative by the young person;

o the young person can maintain a higher degree of responsibility for his/her actions;

o the young person can maintain contact with his/her own community;

o the young person is not being placed with older offenders with the subsequent risk of being trained in crime.

How the scheme works

Youth justice workers call a planning meeting within 24 hours of placement with foster parents.

This is attended by the youth justice worker, the carer, the young person, parents, the case holder and a social worker from the Social Services Fostering Section.

The purpose of the meeting is to agree a contract between the foster parents, the young person, the young person's parents and youth justice staff. The contract specifies the circumstances of the remand and any associated problems, the expected duration of the placement, agreed objectives, contact between the young person, parents and youth justice staff, the levels of supervision by the foster parents, house rules and expectations, the financial payment to the carers and the levels of support they are offered.

Each party is given a copy of the contract. If there is any breach, the meeting is re-convened.

Results

The scheme was reviewed during a three-month period in 1991. Although it had not been operating long enough to allow for extensive results, the subsequent report concluded:

'Parents and social workers consulted said they believed that the scheme has achieved a measure of success in stopping/reducing offending for the period of the remand episode. 6 out of 8 young people said they had stopped offending or cut down whilst living with foster carers.'

Remand Foster Placement Contract

1. I understand that I have been placed on Remand and will live with Remand foster-parents so long as I comply with demands outlined below or until my legal situation changes.
2. I will remain under 24-hour supervision until after my first planning meeting which will be held within . . . . . . hrs.
3. I agree that I will co-operate with my foster parents by:
   a. not committing any further offences.
   b. attending court when required.
   c. respecting the house/family rules.
   d. attending school/work as and when required.
4. I will keep all my appointments with Kirklees Juvenile Justice staff.

It has been explained to me that if I fail to keep to this agreement that my placement will be reviewed and I may be placed in residential care.

Signed: _____

Young Offender Community Support Team, Fareham

Young Offender Community Support, 32a Ceder Road, Inner Avenue, Southampton SO2 0HL
Telephone: Southampton (0703) 322372

'It's an opportunity. Somewhere stable to live. I got into a bit of trouble before, while I was living in children's homes, but now I don't feel I need to go out stealing cars.' Young Person

'When I first read about the scheme I thought, 'Who in their right mind . . . !' But as I became more involved and understood more about what the scheme was about and the support available I realised that it is an invaluable resource. It gives offenders an opportunity to rebuild their lives in a 'normal' environment which will address their individual needs. If they're prepared to make the commitment then it's probably the best way of dealing with them.' Carer

'The partnership is a "smart" crime and custody prevention initiative which, in my experience, has successfully harnessed the raw energy, concern and commitment of the carers to good effect. Placements can demand a more intensive investment by supervising Probation Officers and challenge styles of working, but the expenditure is, in my view, most cost effective.' Probation Officer

'This scheme is a welcome addition to the range of options available to a sentencer. It has the particular attraction to a sentencer that the support being offered is there all the time. It has the second attraction that it shows the young person that people really do want to help him or her in a positive way.'

Sentencer (His Honour Judge Wroath)

Voices from the Young Offender Community Support
Scheme Annual Report, 1991–92

Background
This scheme has existed since 1989 and replaces the use of custody for 16–21 year olds with placement in a foster home. It operates as a partnership between the National Children's Home (NCH), Hampshire Probation, the young person and the support family.

It aims to provide a supportive home environment and to encourage the young person to work with the Probation Service to confront the offending behaviour, to develop more responsible ways of dealing with problems and to make constructive plans for the future.

The project operates on the following principles:

○ custody is a negative experience which only leads to re-offending;
○ periods of custody are likely to accelerate a person's criminal behaviour;
○ the service should be available to all, regardless of race, gender, disability or sexuality;
○ the individual has a right to make decisions affecting his/her lifestyle; and
○ the project gives consideration to the needs of the victim, the community and society.

How does the scheme work?

The project recruits supportive families who will provide accommodation either for a period of bail or as a condition of a probation order.

A study of the scheme published in May 1993 by the Dartington Social Research Unit found the carers come from all walks of life and cover a wide range of ages, family composition and socio-economic status. Some are ex-offenders, some have religious motivation (NCH is affiliated to the Methodist Church) and most want to provide a community service by helping to prevent crime and enabling the offender to become reintegrated into society.

A conscious effort has also been made to recruit families from a range of ethnic backgrounds.

The recruited families are paid to provide accommodation and physical and emotional support. Each family must undergo a period of training covering aspects of work with young offenders including the problems they will encounter in the work, safety for their own family members, health education, anti-discriminatory practice and how to ensure the young person's independence.

Following the initial training, each family is subject to checks from the police, Social Services and their GP. Personal references must also be provided.

If no problems arise, the family must then go before a vetting panel for final approval. This is not a scheme for those who simply want a lodger!

Room does exist for an element of choice. During the initial stages of placement, the young person's views are sought about the suitability of the family.

After placement, the family is visited weekly by the project staff and a monthly meeting takes place between the young person, the probation officer, the family and project staff to review progress and ensure all parties are clear on the aims and objectives for the coming four weeks.

Case Study: Sandy living with Mr and Mrs Smith

Sandy spent much of her childhood in local authority care after problems between her and her mother made it impossible for her to stay at home. Sandy has very unhappy memories of this period. She talks about the disappointment of not seeing her mother, and of feeling lonely, despite the residential staff trying hard to help her.

After leaving care, Sandy abducted a child. She was found shortly afterwards with the baby safe and sound, was interviewed by the police and subsequently remanded to prison. She spent two days there and was kept in the hospital wing for protection.

During those two days, her probation officer found her a bail address and, upon returning to court, Sandy was granted bail with the condition that she reside at a bail hostel.

At the hostel, the probation officer introduced Sandy to the Community Support Team who began arranging a placement. Sandy felt she could not meet the expectations of the first family to whom she was introduced and, following a further short stay at the bail hostel, she was introduced to Mr and Mrs Smith.

On the day they met, the family outlined their rules and expectations. The rules were simple: to be honest, respectful and not to view their home and the scheme as an easy alternative to time inside.

Sandy talked about her background and the offence and, after a cup of tea 'in mugs – not the best china – which would have turned me off', Sandy and Mrs Smith went shopping.

Living with the Smiths meant being a member of the family – not a lodger. This meant new ways of behaving for Sandy. Thinking back to their first meeting, Sandy comments on how easy Mr and Mrs Smith were to talk to, that they did not make moral judgements and that she could relax with them.

Sandy moved in with the Smiths after her bail conditions changed. When she appeared at the Crown Court, her probation officer gave evidence of the improvement in Sandy's behaviour following the move. Sandy received a 2 year probation order with conditions, including that she reside with the Smiths.

Sandy explains that one of the difficulties of living with the Smiths was learning to talk through problems. The experience of her own family was of problems being resolved by a slap or punch, rather than discussion and compromise.

Mrs Smith speaks of how much progress Sandy has made in being honest and having the patience to sit and talk over problems rather than lose her temper.

Sandy no longer lives with the Smiths, but they are in weekly contact with Sandy, helping out with shopping and other tasks.

Some Questions answered

1. **Do I get a key?** Probably not immediately. Some families have said that they would be willing for you to have a key when they know you better.

2. **What time do I have to be in at weekends and during the week?** This will be discussed when you meet your family. Times during the week will depend upon the family's work commitments and whether they have children. Most families have said that they are prepared to discuss weekend times, depending on your plans.

3. **Can I smoke, and if so, where?** Again, this will be discussed when you meet your family. We need to know whether you smoke so that we don't try to place you with a family who would not want you to smoke at all.

4. **How much privacy do I get?** All families are offering a single room as your accommodation. The facilities in the room may vary, but most families are prepared to allow you your own space as well as welcoming you into other areas of their home.

5. **Can I have my friends round?** Most families have said that they would be happy to meet your friends but feel that, to begin with, this should only be one at a time until they get to know both you and them better.

6. **Can my friends stay?** It is unlikely that any family will allow you to have a friend stay overnight. This is more for their own Insurance purposes than for any other reason.

7. **How would you react if I lost my temper?** It is difficult to answer this on a general basis. It would probably depend upon the reasons why you had lost your temper, but we're sure that all our families will be prepared to listen so it will be important that you try to explain what had happened as best you could.

8. **Can I have my girlfriend/boyfriend round?** The answer to that is similar to that above relating to having friends round.

9. **Can they stay?** Again, the answer would be 'No' for the same reasons as those explained above in Question 6.

10. **How much about me will the family know?** We feel that it is important that the family know as much about you as possible so that they've got some understanding of your life and your circumstances. This will help them to get to know you more quickly.

11. **How much about the family will I know?** You will know all the information about the family which is relevant to your placement with them.

12. **Do I have to go to, or remain with, a particular family?** You can refuse to go to a family or ask for the placement to end at any time. If you are not happy, talk to your Probation Officer before the situation gets out of hand.

Case Study: Kevin, aged 18.
Current Offences: Theft x 2 (mail and mountain bike). Deception x 2 (money from brother's bank account). Attempted deception. Failure to surrender. Breach probation
Previous Offences: 1989 theft of moped. 1990 theft 18 months probation order. 1990 burglary x 2, theft 2 years probation with condition to breach probation) reside at bail hostel.
Referred by: Dickson House Bail Hostel

Kevin is the only black member of a white family. His mother has had a series of relationships, and he has a stepfather and two stepbrothers.

The family are well known to Social Services and Kevin spent various periods of his childhood in care at different children's homes. Consequently, his education suffered and he left school at fifteen and a half with no formal qualifications, having been expelled for persistent truanting.

At referral, he had had a series of manual jobs, none lasting longer than two months, and this reflected his unsettled lifestyle.

He also denied his colour and would describe himself as white.

A placement was recommended with the aim of providing a safe, stable environment in which Kevin could be given time and space to:

a) come to terms with his racial origins;
b) look at his offending behaviour and the causes behind it;
c) learn to trust; and
d) begin to look at employment and future prospects.

Kevin was given a two-year probation order with a condition of residence with a family on the scheme and a condition to attend the 114B programme.

Outcome of the placement
All who know Kevin describe him as a different person. He has not re-offended and obtained employment as a kitchen porter over the Christmas period.

He still resists taking full responsibility for himself and examining his past behaviour and relationships, but this time he has not physically run away from this challenge, which was the pattern of his previous behaviour.

He has shown an increased maturity in his reactions to problems and has agreed to talk openly about himself and the placement to a TV interviewer.

Results

Between May 1991 and December 1992, 55 young people were referred to the scheme. Thirty-one were accepted and placed, one was accepted but never placed, and the remainder were considered unsuitable. The Dartington study traced 21 young people who went through the scheme during the above period. All but four of these were white males aged between 17 and 19 at the time of placement, two were aged 17 and 18 and of mixed race and two were white females aged 17 and 19.

According to the study:

> . . . the majority of young people with whom the project dealt displayed a cluster of difficult behaviours. Almost all had experienced poor relationships with their immediate families, leading to numerous disruptions and moves, including periods of sleeping rough. They had committed a number of offences against property, many of them opportunistic, and sought quick excitement or financial gain. About half were known to abuse alcohol or drugs; five had been homeless at one time or another, and only two appeared to have experience of full-time employment.

The project deals with young people whose emotional and social development is severely damaged: no matter how effective its approach, it is inevitable that a number of the participants should find it impossible to cope with the demands of family life and leave abruptly or re-offend.

The length of placements ranged from five days to nine months. Eight young people remained in their first placement until it reached its planned conclusion; thirteen left prematurely. Five were re-admitted to the scheme after the break-down of a first placement.

The study concluded:

> Half the young people who were placed on the Scheme had

spent periods in prison or youth custody. In fact, those teenagers who were admitted to the Scheme from remand had to wait a considerable time before a placement could be agreed and arranged, thereby weighting the odds even more heavily against success . . .

One young man was placed on the Scheme while on bail, and then given a custodial sentence. His placement only lasted four days . . . Six young people (five men and a woman) have not been charged with a further offence since they were admitted; a seventh, for whom little information is available, is unlikely to have re-offended. The time they have remained out of trouble ranges from 10 to 18 months. Of the remainder, five were charged with further offences while living with foster carers; eight others have been charged with offences since leaving the Scheme. With the odds so much stacked against them, the finding that one third of these persistent and vulnerable young offenders have so far resisted continued anti-social behaviour must be seen as a credit to the Scheme . . .

Seven (of those referred to the Scheme but not accepted) were traced. All but one have continued to offend: five have received custodial sentences for offences committed after the referral and four are currently incarcerated. Only three of the twenty-one young people on the Scheme have been charged with three or more offences since referral, while the same is true of five of the seven who did not benefit from placement . . .

Headstart, Hertfordshire PACT

Probation Office, 1st Floor, 26–28 Church Road,
Welwyn Garden City, Hertfordshire AL8 6PW
Telephone: Welwyn Garden (0707) 329275

PACT stands for Positive Action Contract. There are a number of these schemes throughout the country involving the Society of Voluntary Associates (SOVA), the Probation Service and the Apex Trust. Their primary purpose is to provide the courts with credible alternatives to custody for 17–25 year olds at risk of a custodial sentence.

PACT programmes emphasise the use of volunteers to befriend and assist the participants. They also provide individual plans designed to break the young person's cycle of offending and to help achieve economic independence. Some of these will be discussed in later chapters.

Headstart takes referrals of young people between 17–24 with employment and education needs who have a medium to high risk of custody.

The accommodation element of Headstart programmes enables young people to live in a secure environment with a host family from the local community while still working with a volunteer.

Here is a case study from SOVA's Annual Report, 1991–1992:

Case Study: Simon

I remember the phone call to the office from the referring probation officer. He's homeless and can't cope with community living, he's vulnerable but very risky, she said.

In fact, Simon had spent 4 months at Feltham YOI and had been in numerous probation hostels from which he had either absconded or been asked to leave. He had been housed by 3 councils, eventually being thrown out due to his disruptive behaviour, spent 3 months in a children's home and lived with a foster family, which was also unsuccessful.

He was due to appear in court charged with attempting to obtain £1,495 by deception. He had many previous convictions.

I discussed the referral with a colleague and decided that although it was risky, Simon was the type of referral the scheme had been set up for. I arranged to assess him with the Apex Trust consultant. Simon was very likeable, honest about his past, articulate and desperate to be given another chance.

It was made clear to him that this was his last chance and that if he did not make a go of this, he was going down. It was essential that the right people were chosen to work with Simon, given his previous track record. He appeared in court the next day and was given a 3 week adjournment to set up his PACT contract.

I took Simon to meet Jane, a Headstart supportive accommodation provider and a single parent with two sons aged 9 and 11. Both Simon and Jane were happy with the meeting: he talked openly about his past and felt that Jane 'did not judge him' like previous landladies. Simon moved in with Jane for a six-month period.

The following week, Simon met with his volunteer, Paula, and they hit it off immediately. Simon said he was experiencing problems with Jane: he felt 'in the way' and that the sons resented him being there. This was put down to his previous bad experiences and his expectation of failure. Jane felt that things were going well. It was clear that Paula would be vital in Simon's completion of PACT and that she could support him through the initial difficult settling-in period.

Two weeks after his accommodation was arranged, Simon was given a 2 year probation order. He was strongly encouraged by the Bench to make the most of the 'fantastic opportunity' that Headstart was giving him.

So far, the scheme has worked well for Simon. I spoke to Jane last week: Simon has been making meals for the family and going out to play football with the older son and they seem to be getting on well. With the Apex consultant, he's looking for a training placement and is interested in accountancy.

Headstart has also received a positive response from those who have provided accommodation and care. The 'Smiths' had David in their home for 6 months. His PACT volunteer, Lucy, met with him at least 30 times during that period to help prepare him for living independently. David moved from the Smiths after renewing contact with his parents and deciding to return to his home area.

Letter from the Smiths, 24.10.92

Dear Lisa,

David's time with Headstart seems to be running out fast, and thus gives me the chance to write on behalf of Stan and I.

Thank-you for giving us the chance to share our lives and home with a young person again.

There hasn't really been any serious problems, has there, and I can see quite a few changes in these past few months.

He has come out of his shell and that surrounding wall he protects himself with, laughs a lot and has a sense of humour.

He has been told that his home is with us for as long as he

wishes. Just to let you know, there will be no change in circumstances after November.

We shall miss Lucy's visits, she is such a bright, cheerful person. But I intend to keep in touch – her next client should do very well under her care.

With regards
Yours sincerely
J. A. Smith

Chapter 6

Community Sentences

Background

For less serious offenders a spell in custody is not the most effective punishment. Imprisonment restricts offenders' liberty, but it also reduces their responsibility; they are not required to face up to what they have done and to the effect on their victim or to make any recompense to the victim or the public. If offenders are not imprisoned, they are more likely to be able to pay compensation to their victims and to make any reparation to the community through useful unpaid work . . .

Moreover, if they are removed in prison from the responsibilities, problems and temptations of everyday life, they are less likely to acquire the self-discipline and self-reliance which will prevent offending in the future. Punishment in the community would encourage offenders to grow out of crime and to develop into responsible and law-abiding citizens.   Punishment, Custody and the Community

Home Office Green Paper 1988

Over the past fifteen years, considerable progress has been made in reducing custodial penalties for young people under 17. There is now a wide range of community sentences open to the courts (see introduction) and a number of successful community based-schemes for young people.

The chart on page 93 illustrates the significant shift in sentencing policy for young people over the past ten years.

The Criminal Justice Act 1991

In 1990, the Home Office published a white paper, *Crime, Justice and Protecting the Public*, which laid the basis for the Criminal Justice Act 1991.

The Act introduced a number of new community disposals while maintaining a concern for the safety of the public. In keeping with the White Paper, its framework placed an

Juveniles sentenced for indictable offences, by age group and type of sentence or order in England and Wales

Age	10–13			14–16			17			18–20			21 and over		
Year	'81	'85	'91	'81	'85	'91	'81	'85	'91	'81	'85	'91	'81	'85	'91
Total number of persons sentenced (in 1,000s)	15.1	9.1	2.3	62.0	48.1	17.2	31.8	30.0	17.7	82.3	84.0	64.7	206.9	211.7	190.0
Absolute or conditional discharge	33	39	52	19	22	32	10	12	25	7	8	15	8	9	15
Probation or supervision order	21	18	17	17	17	20	10	12	16	8	11	13	6	7	8
Fine	20	16	9	32	25	14	49	40	28	47	42	37	49	43	39
Community service order	-	-	-	-	4	5	10	12	13	11	14	15	5	7	8
Attendance centre	19	22	21	16	16	17	2	4	5	1	2	2	0	0	-
Care order	8	4	1	3	2	0	0	0	-	-	-	-	-	-	-
Young offenders institution [1]	-	-	-	12	12	8	15	18	11	11	22	16	-	0	-
Imprisonment fully suspended	-	-	-	-	-	-	1	-	-	6	-	-	12	12	10
Imprisonment partly suspended	-	-	-	-	-	-	-	-	-	-	-	-	-	2	1
Imprisonment unsuspended	-	-	-	-	-	-	2	-	-	9	-	-	18	19	18
Otherwise dealt with	0	1	1	1	1	3	1	1	2	1	1	2	1	1	2
Total immediate custody [2]	-	-	-	12	12	8	17	18	11	20	22	16	18	21	18
Total community sentence [3]	40	40	37	32	38	42	22	29	34	20	26	30	11	14	16

(1) Includes detention centre orders, youth and borstal.
(2) Partly suspended and unsuspended imprisonment and detention in a young offender institution.
(3) Probation order, supervision order, community service order and attendance centre order.

emphasis on sentences which match the seriousness of the offence rather than the defendant's previous record.

The Act made a number of other significant changes:

o it abolished the prison sentence for 14 year old boys and made 15 the minimum age for both sexes;

o it reduced the maximum term of detention for a 17 year old in a young offender institution to 12 months;

o it increased the minimum period of detention in a young offender institution to 2 months;

o it replaced the Juvenile Court with the Youth Court and extended its jurisdiction to people under 18; and

o it introduced a new scheme for post-custody supervision.

The Home Secretary, however, announced proposals at the 1993 Conservative Party Conference which back-tracks on some of this progress. He proposed to:

o to introduce a new Secure Training Order for up to two years for persistent juvenile offenders aged 12 to 14 years;

o to double the maximum custodial sentence in a Young Offender Institution for 15 to 17 year olds from one to two years.

This chapter examines some of the community sentencing options open to the Youth Court.

The projects chosen represent a high standard of practice in providing community penalties. The projects offer an individual approach to the young person's offending behaviour by dealing with the seriousness of the offence for the young person and the public at large. They also offer a quick response to the needs of the defendant and the Court, both before and after sentence. Some were chosen because of their sensitive approach to race and gender issues.

It was not possible to deal with combination orders because, at the time of writing, they had only been in operation for a few months.

The supervision order: Surrey Youth Justice Team

Surrey Youth Justice Team, Sherrats House, Mayford Green,
Woking , Surrey GU22 0PP
Telephone: Woking (0483) 723922.

Background

Supervision orders may be imposed upon any young person aged 10 to 17 inclusive and have become a major alternative to custody for older teenage boys. These orders are considered more appropriate for younger people than probation orders which are more designed to reflect the social, emotional, physical and intellectual status of adulthood.

The use of supervision orders remained fairly stable during the 1980s. Their proportionate use declined slightly for 10–13 year olds between 1981 and 1991: from 21% to 17% in the case of males and from 26% to 21% in the case of females; and for 14–16 year old females from 25% to 18%. But it has gone up for 14–16 year old males from 17% to 20%, reflecting the conscious attempt by youth justice workers to develop the orders as an option for more serious offenders.

In October 1992, the Home Office, Welsh Office and Department of Health published national standards for the implementation of supervision orders based on three objectives:

- to assist the young person develop towards a responsible and law-abiding life;
- to protect the public from harm; and
- to prevent the young person from committing further offences.

A young person on a supervision order is placed under the direct supervision of a designated individual who is empowered to insist the young person:

- lives at a particular address for a specified period;
- attends a specified place at specified times; and
- takes part in specified activities.

A supervising officer has the following additional functions:

○ motivating and assisting the young person to change for the better and become a responsible and law-abiding member of the community;

○ helping the young person resolve personal difficulties linked with offending and to acquire new skills;

○ challenging and encouraging the young person to accept responsibility for the offending and its consequences; and

○ securing the young person's co-operation and compliance with the supervision order and enforcing its conditions.

As discussed in the previous chapter, the Surrey Youth Justice Team is an inter-agency service managed jointly by Surrey Probation Service and Social Services. Because a supervision order is a high tariff disposal for use as a direct alternative to custody, the Surrey team is keen to ensure that the order's worth is not devalued and that it is used in a positive way to respond to offending behaviour.

How it works

Team meetings are held weekly to discuss whether suitable cases are recommended for a supervision order. These meetings involve all the staff. The benefits of sharing the information means that the views of probation officers and social workers combine to produce a consistent approach to the courts.

Before a recommendation is made to the court, the legal basis of the order, the reporting expectations, the consequences of a breach and the role of the supervising officer are all explained to the young person and his/her parents.

A plan outlining the broad objectives of the supervision order is then developed with the agreement of the young person and included in the pre-sentence report.

There is a meeting between the young person and the supervisor within five working days of an order being made. The young person is given a copy of the supervision order, the expectations of which are fully discussed. Additional written information is provided which includes the expectations, procedures for discharge, breach and complaint. The young person is then asked to sign the supervision order. These meetings last from 45 minutes to 2 hours.

A young person on supervision in Surrey must meet the supervisor at the venue specified in the information. These meetings are weekly for the first three months, a minimum of fortnightly for the next three months and then a minimum of monthly until the end of the order.

These reporting sessions examine the reasons for committing the offences and attempt to provide practical solutions for problems such as lack of money, homelessness and addiction. There is a particular emphasis on how young people can change their own established offending behaviour.

The Youth Justice Unit also places great emphasis on working in partnership with parents. The young person is therefore visited at home and parents or carers seen if the supervising officer thinks there is still a degree of dependency. These meetings take place within the first month of the order and a minimum of quarterly thereafter.

This can be very useful in improving relationships between the young person and his/her parents and between the parents and the service. These meetings also enable the parents, the young person and the supervising officer to review the order and to ensure that parental support is fully utilised.

The second significant feature of supervision is the work plan.

A clear and simple plan is vital to the success of the order because it outlines an agreed, individual programme with a timetable for identified targets. Each plan also identifies problems and individual needs and looks at the risk of further offending, danger to the public and the young person.

Within the first month, the original plan included in the pre-sentence report is reviewed and altered as required. It is then reviewed every three months.

Work with outside agencies (e.g., for alcohol abuse) can also constitute a key part of the order. If the young person is in local authority care, the supervising officer will establish three-way meetings between the young person, the supervising officer and the social worker. These meetings ensure a degree of continuity and consistency between all who have a responsibility for the young person.

Termination of the order

Early termination of an order is sought if, by halfway, the young person has co-operated with the scheme and has not re-offended. This is in accordance with a basic principle of good practice: that the effectiveness of a supervision order is generally established within the first 3 or 4 months. Long orders are neither helpful nor easily managed by the young person.

If the above criteria have not been met, a termination application may still be made to the court if the supervising officer feels the objectives have been met and there is no significant risk of further offending.

If the court refuses an application for early termination, a further application will not be made for 3 months.

Overall, this practice is in the spirit of the Criminal Justice Act 1991 and its arrangements for the early release of prisoners.

Breach Procedures

Staff at the Youth Justice Unit make it very clear to the young people that a supervision order is enforced by law. This is established during pre-court discussions of the expectations of the order. However, it is important for staff to recognise when the order cannot be enforced and to respond appropriately.

In the event of an apparent failure to comply, the Youth Justice Unit requires an explanation from the young person within two working days. The supervising officer records the young person's explanation (or lack of it) and determines its acceptability.

If the explanation is unacceptable, an oral warning is given. There is a written warning if a second incident occurs within 3 months, but an oral warning if it is after a longer period. Breach action starts immediately if a third incident occurs.

Supervision orders with specified activity orders

Hampshire Youth Justice Service

180 Culver Road, Basingstoke, Hampshire RG21 3NL
Telephone: Basingstoke (0256) 20766

Background

The court also has the power to impose additional requirements with a supervision order. These requirements are also subject to national standards and are intended to focus on the specific needs of the young person.

Requirements can be imposed for a maximum of 6 months. Of the 5,979 supervision orders imposed on 10–16 year olds in 1991, 25.5% had requirements added, mainly to comply with directions from the supervisor.

As will be discussed in Chapter eight, the Hampshire Youth Justice Service assumed responsibility for the provision of all juvenile offender services after 31 May 1987.

This service has developed credible alternatives to custody through the development of structured specified development programmes. Each programme is individually constructed to meet the young person's particular circumstances. It primarily focuses on reviewing the offending behaviour with a lesser emphasis on independence skills and the constructive use of leisure time.

A number of key principles are followed:

o proposed specified activity programmes should be discussed pre-court within team meetings so that agreement is reached on the length and content of the recommendation and who will be responsible for implementing and co-ordinating the programme;

o the plan for specified activity should be attached to the pre-sentence report and should have the young person's consent;

o the programme will be implemented the day the order is made;

o the programme must focus on the offending behaviour

and, with the young person, must seek to identify strategies to reduce the offending behaviour;
o staff will vigorously follow up non-attendance;
o the programme should identify the minimum social work required;
o the programme will have a time limit;
o the service should retain an optimistic view of young people;
o the programme should contain regular reviews;
o the views of the young person and the parents/carer should be considered at all times.

Case Study: Alan
Alan was 16 when he appeared in court in October 1991. He faced eight charges of burglary, assault and theft, with 38 similar offences taken into consideration. He had been before the court twice in the previous 18 months for arson, burglary and theft.

Alan had started getting into trouble when he was 12 when life was 'boring'. He says he attended various youth clubs and church groups but did not find them exciting. He started to make friends with older lads and, from there, to break the law. He first went before the court when he was 14.

Alan expected to receive a custodial sentence at his October appearance. He was worried he might be sent to Feltham Young Offender Institution because he feared reprisals for having hit a police officer. He also feared he might lose his temper and hit a prison officer.

However, the court imposed a 12 month supervision order with the following specified activity programme:

Session 1 General introduction, review expectation of the order, make up a file and outline the county's open file policy. Discuss breach proceedings and undertake exercise one, 'Who is Alan?'
Session 2 Assessment of how Alan sees his offending and how others see him.
Session 3 Start identifying all the offences committed and those that illustrate changing patterns of offending.
Session 4 Detail a number of significant offences, how the offence happened, what roles did others play, when Alan could have avoided getting involved.
Session 5 What are the gains and losses from the offences.

Session 6	Exploring why other people are involved with the offences, peer-group pressure and learning the trade.
Session 7	The police, why they do their job, personal experiences and feelings.
Session 8	Independent skill training.
Session 9	Review of social situation, accommodation needs and relationship with girlfriend.
Session 10	Joint meeting with landlord to discuss accommodation needs and to resolve issues of finance.
Session 11	Review progress.
Session 12	Examine the relationship between the social situation and Alan's offending. What must change?
Session 13	Outline an action plan to work on these changes.
Session 14	Go through action plan again and set targets.
Session 15	The reality of prison. Video on Swansea Prison.
Session 16	Social skills session.
Session 17	'How am I surviving?' Go back to the offending pattern and review personal progress.
Session 18	A review of Alan's parents being burgled.
Session 19	A session about family relationships.
Session 20	A session on emergency accommodation.
Session 21	Review of the supervision order and specified activity programme.
Session 22	Drugs advisory service.
Session 23	Drugs advisory service.
Session 24	Social skills.
Session 25	Management of anger.
Session 26	Management of anger.
Session 27	Assist at the Learning for the Disabled Club.
Session 28	Assist at the Learning for the Disabled Club.
Session 29	Planning for the future.
Session 30	Final review and evaluation.

Alan was required to attend three times per week for ten weeks. The sessions normally lasted two hours. His views on the specified activity programme are revealing.

Question: Was it easier than going to prison?
Answer: No, I had experienced secure accommodation and coming here was tougher. It was no trouble in secure – everything is done for you. Out here, it's harder because you have your own responsibilities.

Question: How was the programme helpful to you?
Answer: I was rebelling against the law but people here were OK. Coming here to the unit has allowed me a second chance and I want to give it a go. In the first week, I was bored but, after I said this, we did different things and important issues like my girlfriend were raised. I started to get on with all the staff and I could talk about why I lost my temper so much. I found the video on Swansea useful. It really showed me what it would be like if I carried on. It showed the games people play and the attitude of the prison officers. The hard thing about the programme was that I had to do it and it all made me think. The staff had a habit of rubbing things in and it made me think.

There are other general features of the scheme. Being on a supervision order involves looking at issues such as management of money, seeking and keeping employment, the use of spare time and leisure activities. Assistance is available outside of reporting times – either through the Youth Justice Service during office hours or the duty youth justice officer.

Personal Monitoring
A separate record is kept of each specified activity and supervision order session. The young person has the right to see the file and state any disagreements over the way in which a matter has been recorded. On completion of the specified activity sessions, the young person is expected to report to the supervising officer.

Failure to comply with a specified activity order is treated very seriously with breach proceedings being implemented in accordance with the National Standards.

Solihull Community Supervision

Solihull Juvenile Centre, Juvenile Court, 8 Craig Croft,
Chelmsley Wood, Birmingham B37 7TR
Telephone: 021 7702534

Background

*A personally demanding, punishing and challenging programme
requiring self-examination and promoting individual change combined with professional support, advice and guidance – an alternative
to prison department custody for 14–16 year olds.*

Community Based Provision for Young Offenders in Solihull,
Solihull Social Services, March 1991

In 1986, one in every seven children appearing in Solihull
Juvenile Court received a custodial sentence. In response to
this, the Social Services Department joined with the police,
Probation Service and Education Department to establish a
range of services designed to reduce juvenile crime and
provide alternatives to court appearances and custodial sentences. Supervision orders and specified activities programmes
form an important part of the Community Supervision Programme and have been very successful in reducing the use of
custody by the Solihull courts.

How it works

A young person facing a potential prison sentence undergoes
a detailed assessment which includes discussions with their
parents. This usually involves a number of visits over a period
of four weeks. In the most serious cases, this may even involve
daily contact between the young person and the youth justice
worker, sometimes as a condition of bail.

Following the assessment, an intensive and individual programme is planned to respond to the specific nature of the
offending and to address any other issues or difficulties that
may have been identified during the assessment period. This
is presented to the court with the pre-sentence report.

Offence counselling is the key component of most supervision programmes. It is designed to challenge and confront the

young person with his/her specific offending behaviour. Such work is painful and demanding and requires emotional as well as intellectual involvement. Through coming to accept greater responsibility for their actions, youngsters are enabled to develop more self-discipline, make more informed choices and to say 'no' when under pressure from friends to offend. It is therefore important for youth justice workers to establish a level of trust with the young people in their charge.

Accordingly, the same person will be responsible for the assessment, the programme, the pre-sentence report and for supervising any order that is subsequently made. The child and the parents will have agreed to participate fully in any programme prior to the hearing. The youth justice worker will be in court to answer any questions regarding the report or the content of the programme.

The following case study comes from July 1991. The Car Offences Group and Woodwork Programme no longer operate as the Centre now tends to buy into other services when appropriate. The second case study, based on a pre-sentence report from July 1993, shows the Centre's continuing emphasis on dealing with the specific circumstances of the individual involved.

Sample Specified Activity Order: Paul, 1 July 1991
The following is a programme of activities designed to challenge Paul's offending behaviour through the imposition of a 40 day Specified Activity Order as an alternative to custody. This programme will last for a period of 6 weeks and has been specifically designed for Paul in response to the nature of his offending behaviour.

The Specified Activity Programme
This is a 40 day programme involving Paul in three individual sessions per week. One session will include offence counselling. A second would include a weekly session at the car offence group and a third session to include work with a sessional worker based at the Juvenile Centre.

104

Individual modules for Paul

1. Offence Counselling

A six-week programme is set out below. This would be specified by the court to ensure Paul's attendance. Also, should Paul fail to attend he would be returned to the court. Each session would take place on Tuesday afternoon after school. The programme is designed to challenge Paul's offending behaviour particularly in relation to motoring offences. Details of this programme are set out below.

2. Car Offence Group

This group is specified by the court to ensure Paul's attendance. Paul will attend the group based at the Solihull Youth Workshops at 7.00 pm each Thursday for the duration of the order.

Paul has a number of car offences and it is anticipated this group will challenge this behaviour in a more appropriate and direct manner than can be done through the first session.

Further details are set out below.

3. Reparation Module

This session is specified by the court to ensure Paul's attendance. Paul would be involved with a sessional worker in a woodwork session constructing an item for use in a local community project.

Offence Counselling Programme for Paul

Session 1
Introductory session
Aims
Importance of complying with sentence
Why do people offend?
Session 2
Victims
How do victims suffer?
Considering feelings
Consequences of Paul's action upon himself and others
Session 3
Self awareness
Assertiveness with friends

How to say no to them
Thinking before offending
Session 4
Violence and anger
Self control
Alternative ways of behaving
Session 5
The police and you
How do they see Paul and how does he view them?
A positive look at the work of the police
Session 6
Leisure pursuits
The future
Setting goals and looking at ways of achieving these goals
Summary of 6 weeks sessions

Car Offence Group

o   Specified activity or Alternative to Custody to develop an interest legally.

o   A behaviour modification course as opposed to reparation, this course is designed to focus on changing behaviour.

o   Specified activity designed to instruct young offenders in the aspects of:

1)   car maintenance
2)   the law with regard to driving a motor vehicle
3)   the importance of tax and insurance liability
4)   penalties in breaking the law
5)   dangers of driving uninsured.

o   The whole package is designed with the principal objective of facing the individual with the responsibilities of driving legally within a framework that does not reward illegal behaviour.

o   Sessions would be divided between Solihull Youth Workshop for instruction on car maintenance and the Juvenile Centre for other components of the course.

o   A qualified instructor could be recruited to fulfil aspects deemed 'specialist' i.e., tax, penalties, dangers to the public, law, dangers.

○ For those youngsters 17 years of age, a further package in conjunction with a local driver education centre could be approached whereby youngsters would attend six lectures that systematically cover road sense and safety issues as well as taking driving lessons which are self paid.

NB. Magistrates would be urged not to disqualify from driving or urged to resist imposing penalty points.

Extracts from 'Martin's' pre-sentence report, July 1993
Reason/s for Appearance:
Take Without Owner's Consent; No Insurance; No Licence; Burglary Other Buildings; Go Equipped; Section 9 Criminal Damage; Theft; Take Without Owner's Consent.

Attitude of Subject to Offending
During interview, Martin made full and frank admissions regarding all these matters.

The offences contained in this report pre-date Martin's last court appearance, when he was made subject to a Two-Year Supervision Order with a 45 day Specified Activity Order attachment.

Since that time, Martin has successfully completed his Specified Activity Programme which involved him looking at issues around his offending behaviour, and a Reparation Module. His attendance has been 100% and he has demonstrated a willingness to work well on the above issues.

Discussions with Martin revealed that he understands the implications to himself and others when he offends. He is aware that if he continues to behave in this way, he may well be at risk of receiving a custodial sentence when he reaches fifteen. I believe that threat is now real enough for him to respond to the plan of work proposed in this Report.

Relevant Information
Martin lives with his parents and older sister. He is in full-time education and currently attends the Lancaster Unit in Solihull.

During this period, he was clearly pushing at the boundaries of parental control.

He was often not returning home from school, staying out

overnight without the authority of his parents and often got into trouble with the police.

His parents were very concerned about his behaviour. They realise that if they are to help him stop offending they need to have a tight control over his whereabouts. They said that his behaviour and attitude has improved. He has kept to the curfew imposed by the courts and appears not to have offended since March.

Martin currently spends Monday evening and Saturday morning with a sessional worker on a voluntary basis. This time is spent promoting leisure interests and offers positive individual attention.

Proposed 60 Day Intermediate Treatment Programme
Aims of supervision and intermediate treatment
1. To protect the public through monitoring of activities and behaviour.
2. To reduce the likelihood of further offending.
3. To offer counselling and support on important aspects of his life.

The following programme is designed specifically for Martin and has three components to it.

1. Sessional Work
Martin is currently working with a sessional supervisor. Under supervision, he participates in woodwork on Monday evenings 4.30 pm–7 pm every week. Martin also sees his supervisor on Saturday mornings. This is an activity-based contact to assist in establishing positive leisure pursuits. Martin enjoys working with his supervisor and participates willingly in both woodwork and activities. His supervisor has reported that Martin is co-operative and enthusiastic.

2. Holiday
A holiday with Rainbow Action Holidays has been organised for the first two weeks in August. The purpose of this holiday is to initially help Martin break the offending networks he has established in Chelmsley Wood and to assist him in distancing himself from the associates with whom he offends. The holiday

will also provide his parents with a respite and they have undertaken to visit Martin midway through the holiday.

3. Family Work

Martin's parents have agreed to undertake work with the Social Services Department to explore issues within the family that may affect Martin's offending behaviour. A programme of 6–8 sessions is planned that will cover issues such as discipline, control and sanctions within the household, family values, family relationships and Martin's family's impact on his offending behaviour.

This work will also enable his parents to take some responsibility for some of the offending due to their own uncertainty regarding care and control.

This proposal was accepted by Solihull Youth Court on 26 July 1993 and the programme successfully completed.

Results

The Solihull Community Supervision Programme has been a great success. Between 1987 and 1990, it succeeded in reducing the use of custody by 50%.

Year	Number in Court	Number Receiving Custody	% Receiving Custody
1986	130	19	14.6
1987	143	19	13.3
1988	178	26	14.6
1989	126	9	7.1
1990	109	4	3.7

Social Services Report, March 1991

There is also an encouraging take-up rate by the courts of supervised activity order recommendations:

1989   16 recommended
           8 made
           8 received custody

1990   20 recommended
        17 made
        3 received custody
1991   8 recommended
        4 made
        4 received custody.

These figures should be put in the context of the overall sentencing trend at Solihull Youth Court which reveals a 27% decrease in all sentences between 1988 and 1991. Of those sentenced, 16 year olds constituted 39% in 1989 and 45.6% in 1990.

Community Service Orders

Kent Probation Service, 58 College Road , Maidstone ME15 6SJ
Telephone: Maidstone (0622) 750934

Background
'At first, I hated it, but I suppose it seemed fair. Actually, it was getting up early on Sunday that I hated – the work was quite interesting. I painted a church hall and then helped make an adventure playground for kids. I'd quite like to do something like it on my own.'   19 year old completing a 200 hour
                                    Community Service Order.
                            Quoted, Kent Probation Committee,
                                    Annual Report, 1991/92

Community Service Orders are made under S.14 of the Powers of Criminal Courts Act 1973 as amended by S.10 of the Criminal Justice Act 1991. They apply to young people aged 16 and over and involve completing between 40 and 240 hours of unpaid work within a 12 month period.

Since becoming available for 16 year olds in 1983, Community Service Orders have established a 5% share of the 'sentencing cake'. In 1991, the rate of breach for 16 year olds was the lowest of all age groups: 12% compared to 19% for 17 year-olds and an average of 30% for all ages.

Before making a Community Service Order, the court must consider a pre-sentence report and be satisfied of the young person's suitability. Like supervision orders, Community Service Orders are subject to national standards which deal with:

o the way in which the order should be managed;
o prompt commencement;
o the rate of work to be expected;
o the standards of performance and behaviour to be expected;
o the need for accurate and timely record keeping; and
o enforcement.

There are a number of successful community service schemes in Kent. During the course of a typical weekend, over 2,000 hours of unpaid work are satisfactorily completed. Accordingly, the Kent Probation Service holds the view that community service provides:

o punishment which does not harm the offender and which avoids the high social costs of imprisonment;
o benefits for particular groups and individuals; community improvement schemes and environmental projects;
o an emphasis on the offender's good qualities which can be exercised for the benefit of others; and
o offenders with a sense of responsibility, achievement and an opportunity to discover hidden talents.

In Kent, community service orders are managed by community service workers from a wide variety of backgrounds. Few have formal social work training. The community service workers are employed in each probation office or in specialist centres like the Medway Centre.

Most of the work is carried out in small groups although individual placements can be made if, for example, the young person has a disability or if gender or ethnicity makes a group placement inappropriate.

The Probation Service also maintains a crèche to ensure single parents have access to community service as a sentencing option.

In accordance with National Standards, breach proceedings are initiated after three unacceptable absences. All workers facing breach proceedings are instructed to report for all work days prior to their court appearance and the bench is duly advised of their response to the summons application.

How does a typical placement work?
A young person convicted of a criminal offence will normally be interviewed by a probation officer who prepares a pre-sentence report.

Community Service may be recommended for anyone whose offence and previous criminal record warrants it. Kent policy is non-selective in method with only the person's health and the need for a settled address being a requirement. It is felt that, where there is no long-term need for probation supervision, it is particularly suitable for those able to respond to a structured, demanding situation, requiring punctuality and good behaviour, coupled with a reasonable work performance under close supervision.

If the probation officer feels community service is an appropriate option, the community service worker will be asked to interview the young person. The community service interview is designed to explain the responsibilities and arrangements involved with the order. An information sheet is provided which the young person is asked to sign at the second interview if consenting to the order.

Community Service Regulations reproduced from a Kent information sheet
Your obligations:
    You must:
    (a) report to the Community Service Officer when instructed to do so;
    (b) work well for the number of hours and as required by the Community Service Officer;
    (c) notify any change of address to the Community Service Officer immediately;
    If you fail to do so you may be returned to court and be:
    1. Fined up to a maximum of £400 and sent back to finish your hours **or**
    2. Re-sentenced for the original offence.

Reporting:
You *must attend* on the day, time and place instructed by your Community Service Officer, fit for work and appropriately dressed.

No alcohol consumption is permitted during community service hours. If you attend under the *influence of drugs or drink* you will be dismissed.

Your supervisor has the *right to dismiss* you at any time *if your behaviour or work are unsatisfactory.*

Failure to comply with these requirements is likely to lead to court action.

The lunch-break is half an hour. Other breaks are at the supervisor's discretion, but no one is allowed to leave the site without permission.

If you cannot attend for work:
Telephone your Community Service Officer in advance and certainly not later than 10 am on the day you are required to work. If your explanation is acceptable no difficulties will result, but failure to provide a proper reason may result in a breach of your Community Service Order.

If you are sick:
You must notify the Community Service Office immediately. A medical certificate is required on every occasion and this must be provided within seven days of your absence. Any absence will be treated as unacceptable until it is proven otherwise.

Finally...
Before you agree to a Community Service Order being made, be sure you can comply with its requirements. If you foresee problems, discuss them before the Order is made, because they could have serious consequences later. You have the right to return to court yourself and to ask for the Order to be cancelled and an alternative sentence passed for the offence. This usually applies only if there have been real changes since the Order was made, but your Community Service Officer will gladly advise you.

Once consent is given, the information is sent to the probation officer who negotiates the number of hours to be recommended in the pre-sentence report.

A young person will normally start work in an adult group of no more than eight people. Each person is expected to undertake a minimum of 21 hours in this group after which time, an individual placement may be considered. Such placements are generally given to older people but their potential is illustrated below.

Case Study: Fred, aged 35
Fred received 120 hours community service for motoring offences and, after completing the required 21 hours within a group, asked to be considered for an individual placement. Given his good work reports, reliability and general attitude, he was considered to be an ideal placement for the Medway Community Living Scheme (MCLS) – a scheme run by Social Services which enables mentally handicapped people who were resident in long-stay hospitals to live in houses as part of the community. Fred was unemployed and therefore able to carry out his community service during the week. Arrangements for the days and hours he worked were made directly with MCLS to suit their requirements. Fred not only proved to be an asset to the beneficiaries, but also enjoyed the work so much that, after completing his order, he continued to work with them as a volunteer. Social Services have been so impressed with his excellent work that they are considering offering him paid employment.

Placements are established prior to the court hearing to enable a swift response if the order is made. The work is carried out both during the week and at weekends, depending on whether the person sentenced already has a job.

The range of placements
Much of the Community Service work is organised through the Medway Probation Day Centre. The following list illustrates some of the group placements available in August 1992:

Fridays
  o Chatham Grammar School for Girls
     A group of 8 painting and decorating classrooms.

114

Saturdays
- One to One Club
  The club provides recreational facilities for disabled adults who are the guests of the community service workers. It offers placements for a maximum of 8 workers who require patience, sensitivity and a caring approach.
- Glencoe Road Junior School
  8 workers decorating a turn-of-the-century building.
- Arethusa Project
  Building an adventure playground in co-operation with the Shaftsbury Homes charity.

Sundays
- The Keep Medway Tidy Group
  Clearing rubbish in co-operation with Rochester upon Medway Borough Council

Individual Projects
- All Saints Hospital
  Assisting with domestic duties, tea rounds and generally helping full-time staff.
- Fort Amhurst
  Working at a local historical monument, including maintenance of grounds, carpentry and electrical work.
- Luton Road – Chatham
  Assisting an elderly lady with a major gardening project.
- Compaid Trust Computer Workshop

The Compaid Trust provides a computer workshop in Tunbridge Wells for people with disabilities. Its premises are within the grounds of the Pembury Hospital where the surrounding areas were initially badly overgrown. This meant adults at the centre could only use the inside of the premises and had no outside recreation facilities. In summer 1992, a group of community service workers completed a major landscaping project which included a barbecue, flower beds easily accessible to someone in a wheelchair, bird tables and a sitting area.

The project took 18 months to complete, with a group of up to ten male and female workers individually completing between 6 to 12 hours per week. Community service workers continue to maintain the grounds.

Trust director, Lorna Ridgeway comments, 'We all felt very safe with the group around and there was never any trouble at the weekends with people breaking into the workshops to steal the computers.'

Plans are underway to develop the landscaping with an emphasis on enabling the disabled people to maintain the grounds themselves.

Extracts from letters from the head teacher of St Marks Primary School and the charity Headway:

> We have been fortunate to receive the help and assistance of community workers since July 1991. All their work has been redecoration. The first task was to finish painting an empty classroom which had been prepared for them. Next they moved to another classroom where they had to prepare the walls before redecoration. At present, one corridor is being 'spruced up' and many favourable and appreciative comments have been made by both staff and parents. We are most grateful for this help – there was no possibility that we could have afforded an interior decorator to do this. The standard of work is high although it does vary from week to week, depending on the supervisor and the men with whom he is working.

> The building of our new day centre at Pembury Hospital appeared to be progressing well. However, what also impressed us was the development of a woodland garden and barbecue beside the Compaid Trust building next door. Our immediate thoughts were about the possibility of our brain-injured people, attending the day centre when it was completed, also using the area in the summer months . . .

> We looked again at our partially built day centre and the awful mess of builders' rubble and the uncultivated area between our building and the woodland garden. The real answer was to have a patio outside our fire escape and a proper path up to the woodland garden . . .

There were about 8 or 10 lads working under the supervision of two officers ... we approached the supervisors and started to talk to them. A few weeks later all was arranged ... in a few weeks time, it will be finished and the result is magnificent. We are grateful to all those who have made this possible and are full of admiration for the workmanship and application of the young people – they are doing a good job.

The Probation Order

Background

A probation order can be issued for any convicted person aged 16 years or over. It requires the offender to be under the supervision of a probation officer for a period of not less than 6 months and not exceeding 3 years.

The Criminal Justice Act 1991 makes the probation order a sentence of the court. It was previously an alternative to a sentence.

Under the S.8(1) of the Act, the court must be 'of the opinion that the supervision of the offender by a probation officer is desirable in the interests of:

o securing the rehabilitation of the offender; or
o protecting the public from harm from him or preventing the commission by him of further offences.'

Here are two examples of projects which deal with young people on probation and which also offer programmes for those on probation orders with conditions. Both projects illustrate how the probation order can respond to the specific circumstances of the offence and the wider causes of offending. Both projects are examples of the voluntary sector working co-operatively with the Probation Service to implement orders for the most serious level of offending.

The Kingsbury Project

3 Kingsbury Square, Aylesbury, Bucks HP20 2JA
Telephone: Aylesbury 0296 397733

Background

Our work is directly aimed at fostering an individual's sense of responsibility and self-worth ...   1991 Annual Report

This project has operated since March 1990 and is jointly managed by the Rainer Foundation and Buckingham Probation Service. It is run by a seconded probation officer with three project workers and administrative support. It is based in the town centre in Aylesbury and the project leader, Maxine Myatt, describes the atmosphere as 'relaxed and easy going ... somewhere that doesn't feel institutionalised and a place where everyone (including the young people) can feel involved'.

The project accepts referrals from the Aylesbury Vale district through the local probation team. It aims to provide support for young people aged 18 to 25 who are subject to probation orders, including those with specific attendance conditions. The staff aim to ensure the young people have safe and stable accommodation and a minimum legal income. This latter task takes up an increasing percentage of the project's time.

An individual approach

The Kingsbury Project's 1991 annual report for the Home Office illustrates the underlying principles of the scheme:

Each young person is regarded as a unique individual worthy of respect and acceptance, despite their offending history, aggression or anti-social behaviour. We undertake to show individuals consistent concern while not condoning unacceptable behaviour. We acknowledge the need for clear boundaries but also a degree of flexibility of response, especially towards a young person who has difficult and negative experiences of authority in the past. We place particular emphasis on sticking by a young person through periods of failure ... in the belief that these themselves can

118

be part of the learning process and that there is always potential for change...

Although the main area of our direct work with young people is to effect change ..., we acknowledge change cannot be imposed and requires consent and motivation. We work on a contractual basis, incorporating the young person's own perspective of their situation in the belief that this is the most effective approach. We also believe that change is more likely to be brought about through promoting and reinforcing positive behaviour rather than focusing on negative behaviour, although acknowledging that the latter has to be challenged...

Our work is directly aimed at fostering an individual's sense of responsibility and self-worth, and assisting them to internalise controls instead of attempting to impose controls upon them.

How the scheme works

As the case study below shows, many of the young people with whom the Project deals have multiple social and personal problems for which there is no 'quick fix'. Many have a history of offending and have served custodial sentences.

An individual programme is devised after a four-week assessment period.

Each programme is designed to reflect the severity of the offence. Some examples of project work include:

- o a project on the effects of driving with excess alcohol and how to get a message across to young people;
- o a project on victims of house burglary;
- o a young ex drug user working with an HIV outreach worker on making contacts with the local community; and
- o a project on independent living on a low income, including survival cooking and economy tips.

A number of group programmes run alongside the individual projects. They include:

- o the Offending Behaviour Programme which is co-led by a probation officer from the Aylesbury team;

o the Anger Control Workshop which consists of 8 sessions covering a variety of situations. It focuses on assertion skills and role plays. Two local police constables join in to discuss confrontations with the police;

o Managing Yourself and Others concentrates upon problem solving, goal setting and communication skills. A consultant psychologist assists with this group;

o the Social Issues/Photographic Group which consists of a small group of young offenders, all of whom have experienced homelessness, and which, working together with a sessional worker, has put together a photographic exhibition and leaflet to assist a local housing action group in a publicity event. Two of the young people involved have also taken part in television coverage of the event.

Case Study: Alan, aged 22
Probation Order with Attendance Requirement for burglary x 2 (dwellings), breach of probation, 19 TICs. 13 previous convictions, including 4 custodial sentences (one of 3 years Youth Custody).

Alan is the youngest of 3 children and was taken into care for behavioral difficulties when he was nine. When he was 15, he was given a full care order because of perpetual stealing and was also abusing drugs and lighter fuel. His subsequent offending was to support a chronic gambling habit. He had a history of conflict and failure within the Care System but despite disrupted education, is considered intelligent and capable of obtaining good academic qualifications.

When he was 18, he formed a close relationship with a young woman still at school who subsequently gave birth to his son. Their relationship survived Alan serving two custodial sentences and a long period in a unit for homeless families, but the couple continued to experience chronic difficulties through lack of income and multiple debts and their own stressed and volatile relationship.

Although the family were eventually housed in Local Authority accommodation, they had few resources with which to set up home. A vicious circle developed in which pressure from debts would impinge on an already fragile relationship and further undermine Alan's ability to hold down employment. (He lost one job when he failed to attend after being thrown out of home and sleeping rough.)

Without work and in a muddle with his benefit entitlement, Alan resorted to further offending for money to 'keep the family together and the debt collectors at bay'. He also had a medical history of stress-related illness and panic attacks.

When Alan was referred to the Kingsbury Project in August 1990, the proposed supervision programme before the Crown Court concentrated on the following areas: managing frustration and stress; employment and budgeting and community work.

From the beginning, Alan made a consistent commitment to the Kingsbury Project and attended almost on a daily basis. He used the Project to gain support in dealing with his family responsibilities and with difficult relationships. He frequently appeared stressed and overwhelmed by the many demands made on him but made a good effort to cope on a day-to-day basis.

He responded well to the workshop with a clinical psychologist on 'Managing Yourself and Others' and developed his communication skills and ability to persevere with problems.

Alan's programme included helping prepare a photographic exhibition for the local Housing Action Group. He also looked at his interest in literature and drama with a volunteer and developed computer skills.

Alan spent much time focusing on employment issues. He was assessed as having the potential to be assertive, extroverted and independent with clear leadership potential. He was interested in catering and the project was able to place him in a trainee position with a local high-class restaurant.

Unfortunately, Alan's pressing financial commitments led him to leave this position to seek unsuccessfully a better paid job.

He was assisted in coping with his acute financial pressures and encouraged to take responsibility for some of the negotiations over outstanding fines, community charge commitments and rent arrears. He was also referred to the Local Authority Budgeting Officer for help with outstanding domestic debts.

Most importantly, the Project helped Alan deal with distressing and volatile incidents with his partner. At one point, she tried to commit suicide after Alan left home.

Alan completed his programme in February 1991 after attending on 82 occasions and has maintained a decreasing level of informal contact.

The difficulties with his relationship remain but he has broken out of the cycle of repetitive offending, is no longer abusing drugs and has not appeared in court for 2 years.

121

Alan's case illustrates the serious and caring approach taken by the Project's staff. This has extended to developing and maintaining links with local judges and magistrates, some of whom have made the following comments:

Sentencers' comments

M.K. aged 20. Sentenced in the Crown Court for ABH, Criminal Damage, Driving whilst Disqualified, Theft, Breach of Probation. 2 year Probation Order with Attendance Requirement to attend the Kingsbury Project. Risk of custody: 95%.

> *Judge's comments:* 'The Probation Officer and all those connected with you seem to think, and I agree, that the best way of ending the vicious cycle of your offending is for a Probation Order to be made with a requirement for you to attend the Kingsbury Project. You have been in custody and you must know that if you continue you will spend a good deal of your life in custody. You can't want this. I will give you this opportunity for the carefully argued reasons given in the report. It is for you to decide whether you can use this opportunity. Probation has not been significantly successful in the past but there would appear to be more of a chance this time. It's up to you. If you commit offences you will be voting with your feet.'

J.M. aged 18. Sentenced at the Magistrates Court for Reckless Drivinging, Theft of a Motorbike, Driving whilst Disqualified, Theft. Two-year Probation Order with Attendance Requirement to attend the Kingsbury Project. Risk of Custody: 75%

> *Magistrates' comments:* 'In total, we have got to sentence you on 16 cases. Several in themselves warrant custodial sentences. People could have been killed . . . theft of petrol from an ambulance is a particularly mean offence . . . but on the other hand, you have only just started offending and you do seem to realise the need for change. We will give you one final chance.'

K.D. aged 24. Sentenced in the Crown Court for burglary (dwelling house) x 3 and breach of suspended sentence with

56 TICs. Two year Probation Order with a requirement to attend the Kingsbury Project. Risk of custody: 100%.

The Judge emphasised that the sentence was a clear alternative to custody indicating that a breach would result in custody. The Judge specifically requested quarterly reports and that any breach be reported to him. After the first quarterly report was submitted, the Judge commented in writing as follows: 'I am very pleased to read the probation report and this report on KD's progress. They are extremely encouraging. I had many doubts before sending KD to Kingsbury. It is still early days, but I look forward eagerly to the next reports. Well done so far.'

Results

The Project commenced at a time when there was a significant drop in the use of custody for 17–25 year olds. Between 1988 and 1990, the number of people aged 17–25 years receiving immediate custody from Aylesbury Crown Court had fallen from 60% to 37%, with a complimentary rise in the use of probation and community service orders. The Project therefore needed to ensure its referrals were genuinely 'up tariff' and that it was being used to strengthen the recommendation for a probation order for young people for whom probation or community service was not otherwise a viable option.

The project has carefully monitored referrals in terms of a number of variables including length of sentence, referral source and outcome and has provided the Home Office with detailed reports of its work for the periods March 1990 to March 1991 and April 1991 to September 1991.

During its first year, the project received 47 referrals, 27 of which were from court proceedings. Of these 27, a full assessment of 19 was completed with recommendations for a supervised programme. The court accepted 17 of these recommendations, one received immediate custody and one received community service. No breach proceedings have been recorded.

Referrals for the period April–September 1991 make up the following overall figures:

Rolling Totals September 1991

Court proceedings	62.3%
Other high risk probation referrals	22.95%
Post-release	14.75%

Referrals (38)

	Crown Court		Magistrates Court	
Age 17–21	11	(29%)	10	(26%)
Age 22–25	12	(32%)	5	(13%)
Totals	23	(60.5%)	15	(39.5%)

Outcome of referrals during court proceedings

38	cases dealt with
19	4B condition
1	4A condition
1	voluntary support
8	custody
4	community service
1	suspended sentence
4	pending

The Himmat Project

Anchor Works, Gerrard Street, off Gibbett Street,
Halifax HX1 5DG
Telephone: Halifax (0422) 348045

Section 95 of the Criminal Justice Act 1991 recognises that 'persons engaged in the administration of criminal justice' have a 'duty to avoid discriminating against any persons on the ground of race, sex or any other improper grounds'. This is the first time the criminal law has recognised this duty.

Probation and Social Services also have a duty to operate an equal opportunities policy. Accordingly, the West Yorkshire Probation Committee states it is an equal opportunities employer which 'endeavours to ensure equality of opportunity in the delivery of services to the public'.

Himmat literally means 'endurance'. The project was established in November 1991 by the West Yorkshire Probation Service and the Calderdale Asian Youth Association. It aims to improve the Probation Service's response to Asian offenders between the ages of 16 and 25 in the St Johns area of Halifax. The Home Office has provided funding for three years.

The pre-trial work of this project is discussed in Chapter three. It is part of the project's function of providing Asian offenders and their families with advice and information on the court process and assisting probation officers with the preparation of pre-sentence reports.

How it works
The project co-ordinator is appointed from within the Asian community and works closely with the Schedule 11 (intensive work) Probation Team which runs a Replacement to Custody Scheme.

The co-ordinator scans the court sheets each morning to identify any Asian offenders unknown to the service. Having made contact with the young people, she can offer advice, interpretation services and support. The interpretation service

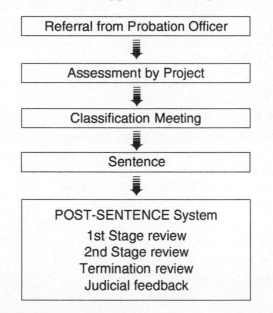

Referral from Probation Officer

↓

Assessment by Project

↓

Classification Meeting

↓

Sentence

↓

POST-SENTENCE System
1st Stage review
2nd Stage review
Termination review
Judicial feedback

is particularly helpful to the families and plays an essential part in ensuring they are supportive.

Following the first court appearance, the co-ordinator contacts the family to explain her duties in more detail. These include offering support in court, assisting with the preparation of the pre-sentence report and explaining the sentencing options.

Experience has shown that both the young person and the family will often find it easier to speak with someone from a similar cultural background.

Young Asians who receive a community penalty are required to work with the project co-ordinator for all or part of the sentence but remain under the supervision of a probation officer who holds the order.

Those under 18 see the co-ordinator with the probation officer or social worker every week.

The co-ordinator will usually undertake the work in relation to the offending behaviour for those on supervision with specified activities. The co-ordinator works with other probation staff in the probation centre or probation office when dealing with those on 4a and 4b probation conditions.

The probation officer, young person and project co-ordinator meet on a regular basis to keep the supervising officer up to date with the order and the individual's progress. These meetings are vital for the project to maintain a high level of credibility with the Probation Service and the courts.

Results

Recent research commissioned by the Project indicates that Asian families often do not understand information from the courts. The Project has begun to correct this and has ensured the probation order is a more positively used option. Young Asians are now less likely to be automatically referred for community service simply because the language or cultural differences made the probation order so difficult to implement.

The inappropriate use of community service meant Asian young offenders and their families did not receive the support and assistance a probation order provides. This is now being rectified.

The co-ordinator also meets regularly with probation colleagues to discuss the project's development and the quality of the services it offers young Asians and their families.

The Probation Order with Conditions

The probation order can be used very flexibly by the courts which have the power to add specific requirements to deal with the specific circumstances of the offending.

Prior to sentence, both the Kingsbury and Himmat Projects specify the conditions upon which a probation order will be made and the requirements which will be placed on each offender. The young person is asked to consent to the order being made and an attendance agreement is reached.

Both projects aim to start work with individuals as soon as possible after court. This reinforces the seriousness and status of the legal requirements of the probation order.

The following projects provide specialist attendance programmes for young adults on probation.

The Edge Project for Young Offenders, Leeds

Leeds Young Adult Offenders Project

The Edge, 11 Queen Square, Leeds LS2 8AJ
Telephone: Leeds 0532 429631.

Background

This project is the product of a partnership between the West Yorkshire Probation Service and the National Children's Home. It has operated for three years and has the stated aim of reducing 'the number of young adult offenders, aged 18 to 21 years, in the Leeds area . . . by providing a community-based risk-management system which replaces custody irrespective of a person's race, gender, disability, religion and sexuality'.

Operating Principles

The practice of the project is based on eight fundamental principles:

   i)   to identify and challenge inequality, discrimination and inconsistency within the Criminal Justice System and elsewhere;

ii) minimum intervention consistent with the needs of the individual;

iii) an acceptance of the need to encourage actively responsibility and self-control within the individual by increasing their available choices;

iv) an acceptance of the fundamental negative aspects of custody upon the individual which further compound offending behaviour;

v)   a belief that a caring and structured approach concentrating on the specific needs of the individual provides the best way forward in dealing with young adult offenders;

vi) an acceptance of a comprehensive systems framework with an emphasis on networking, inter-agency co-operation and liaison in an attempt to achieve consistency and equality;

vii) an appreciation of the specific needs of the victim, community and society;

viii) a commitment to a partnership between NCH, the Probation Service and the young adult offender.

How the Project works

A young person referred to the Project will be seen first by the team manager who will consider suitability in the light of the seriousness of the offence.

Suitable candidates are then presented to the team meeting and allocated an individual officer to undertake assessment if all of the team agrees to accept the referral.

The assessment process involves a 'systematic look at the inter-related issues which can have a direct bearing on offending behaviour'. This is achieved through a series of face-to-face meetings with the young adult which may be held in the home, within the unit or within the remand unit of the prison.

The next step is the clarification meeting. Where possible, this involves the young adult, the probation officer and the project staff member responsible for assessment. This may not always be possible if the young adult is remanded in prison.

The purpose of this meeting is to discuss the information regarding the offences, clarify the respective roles of the probation officer and the Edge staff and to make it clear to the young adult what would be expected if placed on an order from the court.

An assessment report is then prepared for presentation alongside the pre-sentence report. The assessment concentrates upon the proposed programme and how it responds to the seriousness of the offence. It also includes mitigating factors.

If the court grants the order, work with the project starts straight away or the following day.

Case Study: David, aged 18

Current offences: theft x 4, burglary x 3

Previous offences:
Aged 14   criminal damage; fined £8
Aged 15   receiving stolen goods; attendance centre 24 hours
Aged 16   criminal damage; fined £20
Aged 17   burglary, theft x 2; probation order
Background at time of referral:
   o   on bail, very unsettled, 6 addresses in 6 months;
   o   long-term unemployed;
   o   addicted to solvents;
   o   in breach of probation for similar offences;
   o   no family support.
After assessment, the following action plan was drawn up:
Week 1
Review after court: meeting with probation officer to reinforce expectations of order
Offending behaviour: review circumstances surrounding the offences; examine consequences of actions
Substance abuse: arrange visit to drug advice agency
Week 2
Offending behaviour: develop ability to exercise self-control
Employment: visit job centre
Accommodation: provide support
Week 3
Offending behaviour: look at points where David could have stopped offending
Substance abuse: review work with drug advice agency

Employment: continue job search
Week 4
Mid-term review: meeting between David and probation officer to
review progress
Offending and victims: two sessions to review offending from victims'
perspective
Week 5
Employment: examine employment training options
Offending behaviour: examine pressures to offend and not to offend
Week 6
Budgeting skills: assess skills and motivate towards careful handling
of money
Employment: arrange visit to training agency
Offending behaviour: examine times David has resisted offending.
Week 7
Offending behaviour: review work done to date
Accommodation: review progress
Employment: review progress
Week 8
Final review: meeting between David, probation officer and project
worker to discuss progress of programme and plan for the remainder
of the probation order

Response to supervision
During the assessment period, there were problems getting David to
keep appointments. However, his response became more positive
once the court case was over.

David was seen by his project worker for three sessions per week
during the initial part of the programme and was expected to make
weekly visits to his probation officer. The specifically designed programme provided a platform on which the probation officer could build
for the remainder of the order.

The work undertaken on his offending and solvent abuse was
particularly successful. David ceased to use solvents as a means of
escaping his problems and did not commit further offences while on
the programme.

David's housing situation also stabilised. He remained at the same
address for the duration of the order and beyond. Towards the end of
the project's involvement, David commenced a placement on a local
employment training scheme.

Results

One of the key features of this project is the extensive monitoring of its operation. Each annual report has been accompanied by a thorough evaluation carried out by the University of Leeds Centre for Criminal Justice Studies. These results provide an insight into the effectiveness of non-custodial penalties for offenders whose convictions could ordinarily lead to imprisonment.

The third evaluation was carried out in 1991–92. It showed the project had made significant achievements. These include:

i)   reaching its target of 75 project orders;

ii)   continuing to attract appropriate referrals. The average risk of custody score for those attending the project was 85.5%;

iii) maintaining a high level of confidence in the project by sentencers. The project improved its success rate in securing positive court outcomes from 45% to 63%;

iv)   increasing the proportion of black offenders on the programme from 8% to 10%. Statistically, there was a complete racial balance between those receiving project orders and those going into custody;

v)   maintaining a strong working partnership with probation colleagues at a practice and management level;

vi)   providing a cost-effective replacement to custody. The notional cost of each project order was £4,265. By comparison, the estimated cost of the average custodial sentence of 21 months, for those for whom a project order was declined, was £23,380.

Reducing re-offending rates

The report's comments on re-offending are particularly pertinent, given the present level of debate on the issue.

The study concluded that:

i)   twenty-four months after sentence, 73% of those who had undertaken project programmes in the first research period had been re-convicted at least once;

ii)   on this measure, the project group did not differ

significantly from two comparison groups of young offenders who had been sentenced to custody in year one;

iii) those who had been on project orders tended to be re-convicted later and to have fewer convictions, on average;

iv) on the basis of the re-conviction study, custodial sentencing was not demonstrably more effective in preventing and deterring re-conviction than was a project order once the initial incapacitating effect of custody was removed.

In relation to these findings, the 1991–1992 Annual Report comments:

'The data . . . suggests that the initial positive effect of the Project is not sustained over time due, in some part, to the vast social pressures which many young people face . . . It is perhaps naïve to expect all offending and social issues to be completely dealt with in a 60 day period. It begs the question, should programmes be longer if the effect is to be sustained over a greater period?'

Ian Brownlee, from the Centre for Criminal Justice Studies, and author of the Evaluation Report comments:

'Our study found no evidence of an abnormal surge in criminal behaviour among those sent to the Project rather than to custody and given this, and the fact that custodial sentencing is significantly more expensive, the case for community-based punishments remains persuasive.'

Anti-Discriminatory Practice

The number of black offenders initially referred to the Project did not match the proportion of black offenders receiving custodial sentences.

The Project therefore took positive action to increase the numbers of black offenders referred to it including:

o   improving the positive images of black people and women within the Project (e.g., using posters);

o   all members of the project team completing anti-racist training;

- increasing the racial mix of the team. It currently consists of 3 black workers, 6 white workers, 6 women, 3 men;
- adopting a positive anti-discrimination statement which is displayed prominently within the Project;
- ensuring equal opportunities programmes are operating appropriately;
- pro-actively seeking referrals (e.g., providing publicity to barristers and solicitors);
- incorporating cultural issues into the assessment programme.

Over the past 12 months, the proportion of black offenders placed on the Project has increased from 8% to 10%. It remains an important issue for the Project. The 1991–1992 Annual Report provides the following case study.

Case Study: Craig

Craig was taken into local authority care in 1985. Certain factors contributed to this outcome, none of which included offending. Primarily, Craig's problems started at the age of 14.

He moved into a new area which involved attending a new middle school. Craig was the only black child at the school and most of the teachers and pupils were racist. Craig was not accepted and found it difficult to cope – problems arose due to prejudice and ignorance.

Craig came from a strict religious background, the youngest of three sons. His two brothers had finished their schooling and were gainfully employed, one being a police officer.

A well-meaning social worker became involved with Craig following his problems at school. It was decided his problems were due to his strict family background and, having heard that Craig had been hit with a belt on one occasion, the social worker convinced him he would have a better life in care. Craig, who was 14 years old at the time, agreed. The order was made.

It wasn't long before Craig realised he wanted to be with his family, especially his mother to whom he was very close. Craig continually ran away only to be picked up at the family home. The authority solved this problem by placing him in secure accommodation with boys viewed as being beyond parental control.

Within one year, Craig received his apprenticeship in offending from the other boys in the secure unit. His first offence of burglary led to two months in a detention centre. His second offence in the same year resulted in six months in a Young Offender Institution.

While Craig was serving his six-month sentence, his mother fell ill and was rushed to hospital. Craig was allowed to visit her and was taken to her bedside handcuffed to a warder. Craig's mother died while he was at her bedside.

Craig blamed himself for his mother's death and was beside himself with grief. Doctors administered tranquillisers to calm him down and continued to prescribe them for one year.

Craig went from tranquillisers to glue sniffing and then to cannabis, ecstasy, cocaine and crack. Craig appeared in court in 1989 and received another custodial sentence in 1990. By now he was a drug addict. It had taken just five years to turn a loveable youngster into a bitter, confused, suicidal young man unable to face reality.

Craig was referred to the Edge in 1991 when he was at very high risk of custody for his current offences. The Project undertook extensive work with Craig, his family and the probation service in order to place an appropriate package before the court.

Craig needed help and support to overcome his addiction and, in turn, counteract his offending. The project was able to secure him a place at a Residential Rehabilitation Centre for Drug and Alcohol Misuse. The project presented the court with the facts of Craig's background, his motivation to tackle his drug addiction and recommended the court consider a deferred sentence of three months in order that Craig could prove to the court he was serious about changing his lifestyle.

The court accepted the proposal and gave Craig the chance he needed. He completed the deferment period without re-offending – although he did not find it easy. Along with workers from the Probation Service and the Rehabilitation Centre, the Project was able to offer support and monitor Craig's progress.

Craig was finally given a two-year probation order with a further three months at the Residential Rehabilitation Centre. Although the disposal meant the Project could no longer work with Craig, it had nevertheless played a positive role in diverting this young man from almost certain custody.

Sherborne House

Sherborne House Probation Centre, 34 Decima Street,
London SE1 4QQ   Telephone: 071 407 2264

Background

'I was explaining why I had hit this bloke because he gave
me a load of cheek when I was driving my car. We went
over the scene again and again. The probation officers were
saying how I could have done it different and not let the
bloke get to me and so not end up in court. By the end of
the session I saw what they meant.'

John, aged 19, talking about the offence discussion groups
during the Sherborne House programme.

Sherborne House is a probation centre in Bermondsey which
provides a full-time scheme for young people who are facing a
custodial sentence. Young people attend as a condition of a
probation order or, in the case of some 16 year olds, as a
condition of a supervision order.

The scheme is for young male offenders aged 16–20, who
live in the inner London area, but who are not in full-time
education, employment or training. The programme is designed for young people who have engaged in serious and/or
persistent offending. Over 80% of the young people who have
used the scheme have served previous custodial sentences.

The scheme operates as a partnership between the Inner
London Probation Service and the Sherborne House Trust, a
voluntary body which provides considerable support and
financial assistance as well as the building in which the centre
is housed.

The staff comprises experienced full-time probation officers
and craft instructors, assisted by part-time specialist tutors and
sessional workers.

The centre caters for 104 participants per year, in eight
groups. Two groups begin each three months. All places are
taken up, costing approximately £72 per week per place. This
compares favourably with custody which costs £341 per week
or more if in a high-security establishment.

How does it work?

A young person referred to the scheme attends twice for assessment. The first time involves a group session aimed at familiarising people with the Sherborne House programme. The second is an individual interview to assess the young person's suitability and to ensure informed consent to participation on the scheme.

Assessment can only be conducted if the defendant has been bailed for the purpose. Whilst a four-week remand is usual, assessments can sometimes be completed more quickly. A written report which sets out the result of the assessment and makes recommendations is then prepared for the court.

The scheme consists of an intensive and fully integrated timetable of group work sessions, craft workshops, life skills training, creative arts including drama, sporting activities and outdoor pursuits. There are daily offending behaviour groups in which a variety of exercises, focused discussions and role-play techniques are used to confront and challenge attitudes excusing or seeking to justify criminal activity.

Anti-social attitudes and behaviour are consistently challenged. Participants are expected to behave with respect towards people of different race, age, sex, disability, sexual orientation or religion.

Participants are placed in a group of up to twelve young people. Most mornings involve a group discussion with two probation officers on offending behaviour. The rest of the morning is spent in one of the workshops where craft instructors help with individual projects such as making furniture or pottery and printing T-shirts. There are short courses in music, photography, computers, cookery and sports and outside activities such as karting, dry-slope skiing, horse riding, climbing, sailing and visiting the cinema.

There is a 'futures' course to help young people plan for life after the scheme. Grants and assistance for equipment can be obtained and advice on small business ventures is available. Those on the scheme can still claim benefit and are allowed time to sign on; 16 and 17 year-olds are paid initial training allowances.

The programme lasts 10 weeks and attendance is required from 10am to 4pm, Monday to Friday. Failure to attend regularly, participate fully or behave reasonably will result in a return to court for breach and resentence.

Results

'Something that keeps me off the street with regular contact and with workers that care.'

'It has to be practical and not just talking. For example, getting help with money, training or jobs.'

A general feature of non-custodial schemes, reflected clearly at Sherborne House, is an emphasis on the views and needs of young people themselves. Staff at Sherborne House have found that young people want practical responses to their problems and can be motivated if they see results. Many have been scarred by previous experiences of custody or care:

'I was sent down when I was 14 and it hardened me – I didn't care any more. My mum thinks I have changed. I have to put on a front all the time.'

'Jail is a stupid place to go. If you are soft, it fucks you up. If you are rough, it makes you rougher and you go out and do more crime.'

'Prison makes you change when you do not want to – it's the only way to survive'.

'Going into care really affected me. I was 14 and I had just committed my first offence – the next year I committed nine. They kept moving me to places where there were only white people. I had it hard.'

A major study of the Centre's work is presently being finalised. It is expected to confirm the impressive results published in 1988. These showed that the re-conviction rate for the 12 months after beginning the Sherborne programme was 36% compared with 54% for young men leaving youth custody. It is important to note that the youth custody figure includes many lower tariff individuals (fewer than 6 previous convictions) and that the Sherborne House figure excludes clients who either failed to start or complete the programme. Nevertheless, this is an encouraging result for those completing the programme.

Other aspects of the research confirm the view that young people grow out of crime:

- of the 81 individuals in the sample, 32 aged 16–18 did not complete the programme compared with 9 aged 19–20;
- 16 to 18 year-olds were more likely to be re-convicted, particularly if they had experienced custody;
- individuals with a high number of previous convictions were not more likely to be re-convicted than those with fewer previous convictions.

Perhaps the final word can be given to some of the young men who were subjects of the research. When asked how their view of offending had changed, several stated in a variety of ways that they did 'not need that nonsense any more' or 'have lost my bottle' or 'I've given that all up – what a waste of time'.

Break-Free (the Haringey Project)

Break-Free, First Floor, South Block,
The Selby Community Centre, Selby Road, London , N17 8JN
Telephone: 081 885 5000

Background
This project was established in January 1993 and operates as a partnership between the Rainer Foundation and the Middlesex Area Probation Service. Its first report to the Home Office was completed in April 1993.

Break-Free provides a service previously unavailable to Middlesex Area Probation Service for young people aged 17–25, who commit serious offences and who are at risk of custody. The service is provided either as a condition of attendance or as a voluntary part of a probation order for Haringey probation clients with special needs.

The new premises form part of the Selby Community Centre and include a large reception area. This has a corner for children's toys to allow for clients who are parents. Break-Free intends to develop a library for clients and presently displays pamphlets and posters advertising other agencies and promoting positive messages and images.

The open-plan office allows informal contact between clients and staff and the kitchen facilities can be used with some clients to improve social skills and cooking.

How it works

Clients are automatically referred by the probation officer preparing the pre-sentence report if the gravity of the offence is four or above on the Middlesex Probation Service risk of custody scale. This means the offence is serious and would ordinarily attract a custodial sentence. The assessment period for the pre-sentence report depends upon the serious nature of the offence and the sentence date established by the court.

If the young person has been fully assessed, the project worker provides a separate report to the court outlining the Project's role, assessment and the programme that could be provided. The value of seeing clients on several occasions during the assessment stage has been shown in most cases by their subsequent commitment to attendance once the order has been made.

If a condition is made, the client is seen either on the day or within 2–3 days of court. A three-way meeting between the young person, the probation officer and the project worker is held to clarify expectations of attendance and the different areas of work to be undertaken. There are regular reviews and all the client's activities are recorded on a file to which the client has access.

Once an order ends, clients are offered voluntary contact if they wish to pursue a particular issue.

The programme is broken down into distinct areas of work including:

- 7 formal group sessions of the Core Offending Programme;
- reparation and/or making a positive contribution to the local community;

○ other issues related to offending e.g., housing needs, social skills, employment and training, constructive use of leisure time, drug and alcohol counselling.

The Core Offending Programme is run by project staff and the Drug Advisory Service with plans for probation staff also to be involved. It operates on a rolling basis so that new clients can join when they start.

The seven elements of the programme are:

○ offending behaviour – the triggers/the process;
○ peer group and family pressure;
○ self-esteem, assertion and role models;
○ understanding the criminal justice system;
○ racism and offending;
○ masculinity and offending; and
○ drug and alcohol use and offending.

Because the project staff know the young people they are working with quite well, individual sessions may be tailored or changed to meet specific needs.

Many of the people using the project have special housing needs. Break-Free provides help and assistance with:

○ liaison and referrals to local housing resources;
○ liaison with the leaving care team for placement with local bed and breakfast accommodation;
○ preparation for independent living e.g., self-care, hygiene, cooking, budgeting and support once in accommodation.

Employment and training sessions include:

○ an assessment of the young person's level of literacy and numeracy, skills level and previous experience;
○ preparation for work e.g., training, CV preparation, job applications, interviewing skills, taster days with local employers.

Constructive use of leisure sessions include:

○ an assessment of how the young person uses his/her time;
○ an introduction to community groups and the facilities at

the Selby Centre;
o taster sessions in canoeing, sailing and rock climbing;
o an introduction to other skills e.g., artwork, drama; and
o access to computers.

During its short life, the team has visited and presented Break-Free's work to all four Haringey probation field teams, the Crown Court probation team, the senior judge and judges at Wood Green Crown Court, the Haringey Youth Justice team and a number of local community organisations.

Results
Break-Free opened for referrals on 15 March 1993 and received 29 over the first 8 weeks for the following offences:

o 9 x domestic burglary;
o 7 x non-domestic burglary;
o 5 x robbery;
o 2 x road traffic;
o 2 x deception;
o 1 x drug exportation;
o 1 x actual bodily harm;
o 1 x affray; and
o 1 x theft.

Most of those referred had committed previous offences – for example, multiple burglary. The theft involved goods to the value of £1,500 while the client was in breach of a YOI licence and the majority of cases were dealt with by the Crown Court.

By the time Break-Free's first report to the Home Office was submitted, 13 full assessments had been completed with the following pre-sentence report proposals:

o 9 x probation order with condition of attendance at Break-Free;
o 1 x probation order with voluntary attendance at Break-Free;
o 2 x probation order; and
o 1 x conditional discharge.

These proposals met with the following response:
- o the conditional discharge and 2 of the proposed probation orders were followed;
- o the 3rd proposal was not followed and the client received a 5 month prison sentence;
- o 4 received probation with a condition of attendance;
- o 3 results were pending;
- o 1 received a combination order with a condition of attendance;
- o 1 received probation with voluntary attendance; and
- o 1 received custody.

Case Study: Jason
Jason was referred by his probation officer on 12 March 1993 prior to his court appearance on 23 March 1993. He was unemployed and bored and had committed actual bodily harm and common assault during an ongoing dispute between himself and his friends and the local kebab shop. Jason had poked his finger into the eye of the kebab shop assistant and caused a tear which needed stitches. Seven days later, he fired an air pistol at the shopkeeper which fortunately missed.

Break-Free saw Jason with his mother at the Project on 17 March and attended court with a short report introducing the Project, referring to the issues discussed but stating that more time would be needed to complete the assessment.

Bail was extended to 13 April and Jason met all of Break-Free's staff during the three occasions he attended for the completion of the assessment. Jason's motivation was high and a good rapport was developed. He kept all of his appointments and even brought a friend who was later formally referred.

The issues identified during the assessment included his denial of the seriousness of the offence, the possibility of it being racially motivated, the need to control his temper and his immaturity, his lack of formal education and possible illiteracy and the need to use his leisure time constructively.

A 30 days attendance order at the project as either a condition or a voluntary part of a probation order was put before the court. The proposed programme consisted of:

- o the Core Offending Programme;
- o as reparation, helping identify ground rules for acceptable client

behaviour at the project and, with guidance, producing a leaflet for future clients;

o   exploring his literacy and numeracy and providing employment support; and

o   taking part in sessions on constructive use of leisure time.

Break-Free undertook to see Jason twice a week while he remained unemployed and once a week if he gained full-time employment.

Jason was given an 18 month probation order with a condition of attendance at the Centre plus compensation and costs totalling £900. Break-Free also undertook to liaise with the owner of the kebab shop over the outcome.

Jason's targets have been set and he has partially completed the programme. Some of his attitudes are being challenged and his motivation remains high. The keyworker also visited the kebab shop and discussed the outcome of the court case and future issues. The victim was appreciative of this and, to date, there has been no re-occurrence of the offence.

Both Jason and the Project appear to have made a good start.

Lewisham and Greenwich Intensive Probation Project

Inner London Probation Service (ILPS),
54–56 Lewisham High Street, London , SE13 5JH
Telephone: 081 463 0036

Background

This Project started on 20 January 1992 and developed out of a 1988 Home Office initiative, 'Tackling Offending – An Action Plan'. The Project provides intensive individual programmes designed with the young people who attend as a requirement within a probation order. It initially targeted the 17 to 21 age range but was extended to include 16 to 25 year olds.

Prior to the starting date, Project staff compiled a list of community resources and visited many centres including Millwall Football Club, Lewisham Music Academy and Lewisham Young Women's Project. Presentations were made to probation centres, courts, field teams in the area and at the Greenwich Court Magistrates' Liaison Meeting. Information leaflets are available for courts, probation officers and young people.

How it works

Initial referral inquiries are discussed with the project probation officer and, if suitable, those on bail are assessed either
during the original remand period or after a further remand
has been requested. It is only possible to decide on suitability
for assessment for those in custody. For a full assessment to
take place, bail must be granted.

The referring probation officer prepares the pre-sentence
report. The project probation officer completes a standard pre-
sentence report and an individual programme for those who
have been accepted. The project probation officer also attends
court whenever possible with those who have been assessed.

Individual programmes are designed during the remand
period. Each programme consists of a one-to-one session with
the project probation officer and attendance at the weekly
Offending Behaviour Group (unless participation in groups is
unsuitable).

The Offending Behaviour Programme is co-led by the project
probation officer and the probation service assistant and runs
one morning and one evening per week. A comprehensive
programme has been designed using such exercises as: gains
and losses of offending; why I offend; courtroom role-play
(using video) and the police.

There are often useful discussions on themes pertinent to
young people: peer pressure, racism, drugs and alcohol and
job prospects. The evening sessions are usually smaller and
tend to concentrate on themes, such as alcohol-related offending,
as they emerge.

Other sessions involve attendance at office-based or
community-based resources. Those in full-time employment
or education are expected to attend a minimum of two
sessions per week and others, a minimum of three.

Examples of individual programmes

A

Attend individual session	Tuesday am
Attend futures session	Tuesday pm
Attend alcohol counselling session	Thursday pm

Attend Offending Behaviour Group	Friday am

B *Full-time employment*

Individual session	Monday evening
Offending Behaviour Group	Tuesday evening

C

Individual session	Monday am
Photography	Tuesday pm
Offending Behaviour Group	Thursday am
Participate in 5 day adventure activity in June 1993	

The programmes are constantly reviewed. Attendance at the alcohol counselling sessions is usually limited to 12 and attendance at the offending behaviour group is monitored. The programme can be changed to bring in new sessions or follow-on sessions e.g., work on the futures programmes may lead to a GCSE correspondence course.

All those accepted are asked to sign a contract clearly stating the boundaries, conditions and sanctions. There is a clearly set out warning system which can ultimately lead to breach action. Where a young person is experiencing difficulty in completing a programme, a disruption meeting is called at which changes can be made if appropriate. Young people can be accompanied by a person of their choice at these meetings.

Staff have found that apart from the Ilderton Motor Project (see Chapter seven), office-based resources have proved more successful than community-based ones such as the Lewisham Music Academy where young offenders have found it difficult to engage in an unfamiliar setting.

The Project is consequently extending its range of office-based resources. A sessional worker now runs the futures session in 10 week blocks exploring the opportunities provided by correspondence courses and charities. Other resources/activities include: a literacy scheme; photography sessions; black empowerment groups run in eight-week blocks by black probation staff and outside activities such as a visit to the opening of the Malcolm X film.

Referrals may also be made to other probation-led initiatives such as the Crossroads Project and adventure activities organised by the Lewisham Resource Centre.

The DUAL team visits the Project weekly to provide drug and alcohol counselling and Reduction Treatment Programmes.

Case Study: David, aged 20

David was initially referred to the Project for two counts of driving whilst disqualified. This was his second time in court on similar matters during the preceding six months. Because of the nature of the offence and the pattern of offending, he was deemed to be in serious danger of going to prison. As David was a full-time student pursuing a course in electronic engineering at SELTEC, he was ineligible for the Sherborne House or other Schedule 1 schemes run by ILPS offering only daytime programmes.

During the assessment stage, David admitted that he had been driving illegally in order to earn his living mini-cabbing. He said he was under some serious financial pressure and that he had 'taken a risk' in using his car. He also acknowledged that he got 'a buzz' from driving and he said it was difficult for him not to get behind the wheel. Whilst acknowledging his responsibility, he added that succumbing to temptation meant that he would break the law.

David's initial programme included attendance at the probation office once a week to discuss his financial worries and monitor the payment of his fines. He also committed himself to working two evenings per week after college at the Ilderton Motor Project. Here, as well as learning mechanical skills, he took part in discussions about safe and legal driving with other young people. To satisfy his interest in driving, he quickly put himself forward for the competitive 'banger' racing that the Motor Project gets involved with at weekends. On Friday mornings, he attended the Offending Behaviour Group sessions where his ideas and attitudes towards driving continued to be challenged constructively by others in the group.

Formally, the IMP offers the end of the line as young people are often facing the prospect of prison. Perhaps this fact gave David the incentive to do well on the Project. He attended regularly and enthusiastically throughout his time at the scheme. He said he was keen to get his sessions finished by September when he returned to college and was pleased when he achieved this aim in October.

When reviewing his progress, he acknowledged that attending the Ilderton Motor Project in particular had helped him stay away from illegal driving. Staff at the project commended David on his commitment and the skill in mechanics he displayed whilst there.

David now attends the probation office once per month to complete his probation order. He has also negotiated with the Ilderton Motor Project to continue to attend there as a volunteer worker.

Results

The serious nature of the offending being targeted means there is a high risk of refusal by the courts. Of the 37 proposals for probation made by the Project, only 12 were taken up. Other defendants were refused bail for assessment.

The numbers remaining on the programme rose dramatically during the second half of the year. However, project staff consider that those who do not complete the programme can still benefit from participation on it. For example, two young men later remanded in custody for further offences attended between 6 and 8 Offending Behaviour Group sessions at which they were challenged about their continued offending by their peers. One of them also revealed the extent of his hitherto unknown drug habit to the project probation officer and is now being assessed for a drug rehabilitation centre.

Hereford and Worcester Probation Service: Programme for Achievement, Challenge and Training (PACT)

Hereford and Worcester Probation Service, PACT,
30–32 Loves Grove, Worcester , WR1 3BU
Telephone: Worcester (0905) 613822

Background

PACT is an intensive six-week programme of supervision in the community for serious adult offenders. It was established in July 1989 as an extension of an earlier Young Offender Project.

The programme is undertaken as a condition of a probation order and must be completed within the first year. The aims of the programme are:

1. to provide a non-custodial disposal to courts for serious offenders aged 17 and above;
2. to provide an intensive programme which addresses offending behaviour;

Programme for addressing offending behaviour

	Week 1	Week 2	Week 3	Week 4	Week 5	Week 6	Week 7
Tuesday am	Introduction to Geese Theatre 1	Offending Behaviour 1	Relationships 1	Addictions 2	Addictions 3	Violence & Aggression 4	Relationships 6
Tuesday	Introduction to Geese Theatre 2	Offending Behaviour 2	Addictions 1	Violence & Aggression 2	Addictions 4	Employment 5	Employment 6
Wednesday am	Introduction to Geese Theatre 3	Offending Behaviour 3	Employment 1	Relationships 2	Violence & Aggression 3	Addictions 5	Use of Leisure 5
Wednesday pm	Introduction to Geese Theatre 4	Offending Behaviour 4	Employment 2	Use of Leisure 2	Relationships 4	Use of Leisure 4	Use of Leisure 6
Thursday am	Introduction to Geese Theatre 5	Offending Behaviour 5	Violence & Aggression	Employment 3	Use of Leisure 3	Relationships 5	Violence & Aggression 6
Thursday pm	Introduction to Geese Theatre 6	Offending Behaviour 6	Use of Leisure 1	Relationships 3	Employment 4	Violence & Aggression 5	Addictions 6

3. to provide an opportunity for offenders to improve their
    skills and abilities and to change in a way that reduces the
    likelihood of further offending;
4. to expand and evaluate the capacity of this service to
    provide permanent and consistent programmes
    throughout the country which remain equally relevant
    to offenders' needs;
5. to stimulate the development of relevant facilities and
    projects on both a countrywide basis and in local teams,
    and to generate the confidence and skills to meet the
    needs of offenders in a flexible, imaginative and
    appropriate way.

Each PACT course concentrates on factors that are directly
or indirectly related to offending behaviour. These include:

1. offending behaviour
2. relationships
3. addictions

4. employment
5. violence and aggression
6. use of leisure

Analysing the Offence	
Individual tells the story of the offence and what led up to it, in detail and in sequence	
	BEHAVIOUR (*i.e., the offence*)
WHAT? (*i.e., what led up to the offence*)	
WHEN?	
WHERE?	
	CONSEQUENCE (*for self and victim*)
WHAT MOOD?	
WHO WITH?	
WHAT OPPORTUNITY?	

The sole criterion for referral to the programme is the likelihood of a custodial sentence. This may be because of:

1. seriousness of offence;
2. previous criminal history (especially previous custodial sentence); or
3. Probation and community service and other options already tried.

Any referral, either from a probation officer who is preparing a pre-sentence report or from a court where the programme may be considered as an appropriate disposal, is assessed by specialist staff. Assessment involves an interview with the offender so that a detailed explanation can be given of the programme and its content, of the contractual obligations of a probation order, and of the action to be taken in the event of any later breach of the order. Experience has shown this to be an essential process as it ensures that the offender fully understands the implications of the order and the court's expectations.

The Probation Service maintains the normal enforcement conditions and makes it clear that failure to comply with the programme and the rules and regulations for attending the

Group Assessment	
	SITUATION TO AVOID
WHEN?	
WHERE?	
WITH WHOM?	
	CONSEQUENCE IF THEY DON'T
FOR THEMSELVES	
FOR FAMILY	
FOR FUTURE	
	RISK OF RE-OFFENDING . . . . .(Score out of 10)

course will result in breach proceedings being initiated.

The Probation Service is also looking at ways the Project can be made more suitable for women.

How it works

Each PACT course will vary slightly depending upon a participant's needs, level of ability and capacity to concentrate.

PACT involves a partnership between the Probation Service and the Geese Theatre Company, who themselves have a successful history of pioneering drama work with offenders and prisoners. (See below.)

During the first three days of each course, the Geese Theatre Company uses techniques of drama and role-play to confront the participants with their offending behaviour and its consequences. This introduction is very successful in breaking down the defences that people use to justify and excuse their offending behaviour. It helps participants develop their own levels of self-awareness, to understand more about their own styles of behaviour and the internal and external factors to which they negatively respond. This is a good foundation upon which the rest of the PACT programme can develop.

It works by getting participants to act behind masks. The masks represent how true feelings are hidden behind a front presented to the outside world. The exercise challenges participants who commonly claim to have no worries about getting into trouble nor concern for hurting themselves or others.

The exercise examines 'fool factors' which are 'events beyond the individual's control' which can lead to offending e.g., the late arrival of a giro which results in a person having no money and therefore offending.

The full programme is outlined on page 148 and some examples from the programme are provided.

Examples

Section 1: Offending Behaviour

The overall aim of the section is to confront participants with the reality of their offending and its implications. Using a variety of exercises, they examine:

151

Authority Exercise: Handling Situations and People

Look at examples of behaviour given below and rate yourself, on a scale of 1 to 5, as to how well you think you handle those behaviours with the people or in the situations described at the top of each of the five columns.

You feel you handle behaviour with that person	**badly**	score 1
You feel you handle it ...	**not well**	score 2
You feel you handle it ...	**just OK**	score 3
You feel you handle it ...	**well**	score 4
You feel you handle it ...	**very well**	score 5

BEHAVIOURS	Friends	Parents & Family	Courts & Police	Probation Officer	Employer & DSS
Expressing yourself clearly to					
Listening to					
Accepting instructions from					
Challenging					
Understanding that person's position					
Asking questions to get things clear in your mind					
Express your liking and approval					
Express your dislike and disapproval					
Express your ideas and opinions					
Asking for something you want					
Standing up for yourself and your rights					
Disagreeing with					
Expressing you anger towards					
Making complaints to					
Taking criticism from					
Dealing with bad feeling and antagonism					

- the function of rules in society, individual responsibility and the problems of dealing with offenders
- why do people offend?
- gains and losses of offending
- the influence of others or the temptations to offend
- critical incidents leading to offending
- values and beliefs in offending behaviour
- the consequences of offending with an emphasis upon victims

Offending Behaviour: Session 5
The purpose of this session is to provide each participant with the opportunity to look in detail at a particular offence they have committed, usually the main offence for which they are attending the programme. By building up a pattern of the offence and the circumstances leading up to it, participants are encouraged to acknowledge the control they have over these events and in particular to identify what alternative course of action could have been taken or different decision made.

After choosing an offence, each participant in turn describes that offence, the details, the sequence of events and consequences. The rest of the group are involved by asking questions that help to build up an overall picture. Questions include – where? when? why? Did you know someone was in the house? Was the car unlocked? What planning/precautions were taken? The description of each offence can be done by acting the event or drawing a series of sketches.

The information gathered is transferred to a chart until a complete picture of the offence emerges. (See table on page149.)

Through discussion, the critical incidents can be identified where another course of action could have been taken and these are also noted on a second chart. Information drawn together in this way is later transferred to smaller sheets for individual participants to keep.

Through this exercise, each participant learns that it is possible to exercise control over events, that alternative strategies can be employed and that offending is not inevitable. This theme is pursued in the next session.

Offending Behaviour: Session 6
This aims to confront and challenge assumptions that certain behaviours are fixed, determinable consequences. There are a number of ways to achieve this but one example is to involve a police officer or an ex-offender in discussion. Both are able to describe from their own experience how relatively minor incidents have resulted in serious offences being committed. An extreme example is the assault that can result in death. Police experiences of offences are particularly valuable to highlight that the consequences, not the intention are significant. Equally, the offender is able to demonstrate that, whatever the intent, the consequences forced the change in his/her life.

Such a discussion, relating the experiences of a speaker to those of individual participants, encourages participants to consider their behaviour more for its potential for serious consequences and not just for what may have actually happened so far.

The remainder of this session is devoted to assessing each participant's ability to change. Using a series of exercises, participants identify those areas of their lives over which they believe they have no ability to change. The purpose here is to help participants recognise their own potential for change or, alternatively, to acknowledge unrealistic expectations. Finally, course members assess each other's ability to change, using the format shown on page 150.

Section 5: Violence and Aggression
Violence and aggressive behaviour is a part of life that involves us all whether as perpetrators or victims and to a greater or lesser degree. We might not physically assault another person, but we might have a bad temper and verbally abuse someone. Similarly, we might never have been assaulted, but we all know what it feels like to be on the end of a tongue lashing. This section is aimed at broadening participants' thinking about violent and aggressive behaviour and at improving their capacity to deal with it. Using exercises and discussion, the sessions will concentrate on:

GOOD PRACTICE GUIDE

- violence
- aggression
- anger management
- relationships between men and women
- authority
- assertiveness.

Session 5 examines how participants deal with authority figures. The first exercise introduces the subject and requires participants to form their own assessment of how well they handle people or situations. This is a difficult subject and a complex exercise for some, so course leaders introduce the exercise by arranging that the first few behaviours listed are rated by the group as a whole. Once participants understand what is expected, the rest of the exercise is completed individually. This exercise allows participants to identify good and poor responses to different authority figures and, through discussion, to begin thinking about ways of dealing with the negative ones.

Course leaders ensure that in the discussion, questions are posed about how people get authority, how do our expectations influence our relationship or contact with different authority figures, why do some people have authority and so on.

Results
A video is made at the end of each course in which the participants have an opportunity to comment on the course and whether it has been beneficial to them.

Here are some of the comments made by participants who finished the course in August 1992:

'The course was better than I expected . . . This is the first time I've looked back and seen how stupid I have been. One of the best bits was the education on alcohol and the problems arising from excessive drinking. I have cut down on my drinking and now I know my limit.'

'The course went deeper than I expected – some of it was really painful. It made me think, gave me different ways to

155

do things and I have been making it work ever since. This is the first time I have been given something really useful . . . and I have been treated like a person.'

The programme is subject to regular monitoring and evaluation to ensure that referrals to the programme and the Orders that are made meet the criterion that the programme remains an alternative to a custodial sentence. The content of the programme is also being assessed by an independent researcher.

The Project staff hope to repeat, if not improve upon, the findings of the Young Offender Project evaluation which showed:

> Over a two-year follow-up period, 68% of the YOP offenders were re-convicted, but 89% of the custodially sentenced were re-convicted. Not only were the custodially sentenced more likely to be re-convicted, they were more quickly re-convicted and more likely to commit more offences in that they had double the rate of second convictions in the two-year period. As a consequence, 38% of YOP attenders, compared with 64% of those custodially sentenced, received a subsequent custodial sentence in the two years.

Research by Colin Roberts
Lecturer in Applied Social Studies
University of Oxford

Geese Theatre Company

Geese Theatre Company, 220 Moseley Road,
Highgate, Birmingham , B12 ODG
Telephone: 021 446 4370

*'The criminal justice system and its institutions will only benefit
from exposure to the kind of imagination and flair that you obviously
possess.'*

Paul Matthews, Senior Probation Officer,
South Yorkshire Probation Service

*'Not only was the play entertaining and very constructive, but we all
(those who dare let their masks slip for a spell) must confess to having
our conscience prickle in one way or another. Believe me, it conjured
up plenty of room for debate that evening back on our respective
wings. An excellent move in assisting us to take a much more critical
look at ourselves, without being made to look worse than what some
of us feel already.'*
Inmate, HMP Full Sutton,
after participating in a play about family
and personal relationships.

*'I was amazed to see the change in the men over two hours. They
grew taller, broader and more open in a way it takes me months to
achieve with a straight art class. I was not only impressed but a bit
outraged that you managed so much, so quickly.'*

C.Chambers, Lecturer, HMP Norwich

*'Geese are actively working to "set the prisoners free" – free from
their "old selves". I have no doubt that the Geese Theatre as part of
the PACT course is a positive alternative to custody, but also that it is
a positive brick with which to start rebuilding lives.'*

D.W.Fryson, Manager, KARE Hostel,
Stourport-on-Severn

*'It has been organised really well. The first three days broke down the
physical barriers, so the rest could break down the mental barriers. I
can say anything in this group. People in this group know me better
than my mates.'.*
Client, PACT course,
Hereford and Worcester Probation Service

Geese Theatre of Great Britain is a touring group working in prisons, young offender institutions and probation centres. Since beginning work in August 1987, the company have toured extensively throughout England, Wales, Scotland and Ireland.

In addition to their work with PACT, they are involved in live performances, workshops on a wide variety of themes, long-term programme work, staff training and week-long residencies for forming and training inmate and ex-offender drama groups.

They are also involved in long-term probation work in the West Midlands, Avon and Staffordshire.

The team of professional actors and actresses are dedicated to the idea that theatre in prison and probation can be a valuable teaching, learning and rehabilitative tool.

The company is a franchise of the highly regarded Geese Theatre USA, formed in 1980 by the expatriate British director John Bergman.

Devon Probation Service: Victim Burglar Group

Plymouth Victim Burglar Group, Elizabeth Court,
Higher Lane, Plymouth PL1 2AN
Telephone: Plymouth 0752 671075

Background
This scheme was established in 1990 for offenders subject to probation orders with conditions in the Plymouth area after similar groups had shown that victims can make offenders aware of the misery caused by house burglary.

The initiative for the group came from a senior probation officer in Plymouth concerned at the high use of custody for burglary and impressed with other groups run by Avon Probation Service.

The scheme relies on effective co-operation between the Probation Service, the police and a number of community organisations including the Victim Support Scheme, housing agencies and staff and inmates at Dartmoor Prison.

The Victim Support Scheme provides access to victims and

passes on information leaflets. Probation officers have played an increasing role in telling victims about the programme.

How it works

Each group consists of four probationers, four victims and two probation officers.

The basis upon which people attend is made clear from the outset. Probationers have to attend but victims participate on a voluntary basis. Most stay and complete the relevant sessions but are free to leave whenever they wish. Probationers attend ten two hour sessions with the victims and explore the effect of burglaries on all parties.

The Probation Service videos each session and employs a consultant to observe each one on a television screen. However, the sessions are confidential with the exception of information raised by the probationers which may be useful for the supervising probation officer.

The first four sessions examine the effects of burglary.

Before being brought together in the first session, the probationers and the victims fill in an evaluation form which is helpful for the later sessions. The two groups then introduce each other before the victims explain how they were burgled and what was stolen.

The probation officer then asks each victim: 'What sort of person do you think your burglar was and what do you think their feelings were during and after the burglary?'

The burglars are then asked to list the burglaries they have done, what sort of person they think the victim was and how they think the victim coped after the burglary.

After these accounts, there are less formal discussions which concentrate on understanding the feelings of each group. At the end of the fourth session, both groups complete questionnaires designed to evaluate how these feelings have changed.

The fifth session is held in Dartmoor Prison where probationers meet prisoners serving long terms for burglary. The aim is to challenge probationers with the likelihood and reality of a long-term sentence. The session is supervised by probation and prison officers but is largely left open to the prisoners.

The next four sessions involve reparation work in co-operation with the Devon and Cornwall Constabulary. Under one-to-one supervision, probationers fit locks, safety chains and other security devices in the homes of vulnerable people – usually the elderly or single parents who cannot afford such protection.

The tenth session is a review session in which probationers comment on what they have gained from the programme. The victims are not usually involved in this session but may choose to have a review session of their own.

Results

An early evaluation in December 1990 of 14 probationers who had attended the group showed that 3 had committed fresh offences of dishonesty – one of which occurred before the offender started the group. None of the fresh offences involved house burglary.

In summary, 71% had not re-offended and 100% had not burgled houses.

At the time, the average period between the order being issued and the probationer starting the group was 8 weeks. The average time spent completing the course was 13 weeks.

12 of the 14 probationers had previously served custodial sentences – some for house burglary. 7 had completed the group, 5 were currently proceeding with the group and one was facing breach proceedings for non-attendance. The final probationer had his order revoked when sentenced for a further offence which had been committed before the probation order was made.

These results are an encouraging indication that a positive non-custodial approach and increased security for the community can be combined.

Kent Probation Service: The Medway Centre

Medway Centre, 55 Green Street, Gillingham , Kent ME7 1AE
Telephone: Medway (0634) 572479

Background

Michael, one of our early Day Centre offenders, spent much time on his programme being encouraged to use his musical skills. KCC have now made an exceptional decision to support him on a foundation course leading to a degree: 'A mixture of hard work and gratitude for being given the chance,' reports his tutor.

Kent Probation Committee, Annual Report 1991/92

Probation Centres offer the courts a demanding, non-custodial alternative for serious offences. They provide 60 day programmes requiring attendance for four sessions per week. These run during the day or until 9.30 pm. Normal supervision patterns then continue.

The Medway Probation Day Centre has operated for over five years and is one of two centres run by Kent Probation (the second is in Canterbury). Situated in Gillingham, it is easily accessible by public transport and receives those whose probation orders include a condition of attendance at a probation centre.

The Centre accommodation includes a large workshop, interview/work rooms, a kitchen/dining room area and office accommodation.

The Centre is staffed by a senior probation officer, two probation officers, two probation assistants, an evening supervisor, a workshop manager, additional tutors, administrative staff and cooks. The workshop contains equipment for woodwork and carpentry, mechanics and various arts and crafts tasks.

The Centre is able to work with a maximum of 22 offenders at any one time.

How it works

Referrals are made by the probation officer during the preparation of the pre-sentence report. People must attend for four sessions each week during a two-week assessment period. The assessment allows the centre staff to assess the person's suitability and enables the person to understand clearly the potential requirements of the order.

Probation officers try and assess the degree of maturity, motivation and willingness to learn in addition to how the circumstances of the offence can be addressed.

Many of those referred have already served community penalties or custodial sentences. Many see the Centre as the last stop before custody.

The Centre's programme is designed to allow two groups to operate at the same time. Each programme has the following elements:

o offending behaviour sessions. These form the foundation of the programme and are limited to eight people at one time. They attempt to analyse why the offences are committed and the damage caused to all concerned and to break the routine of offending;

o life and social skills, concentrating on aspects of personal development, negotiation skills and practical skills such as budgeting and cooking;

o practical skills such as carpentry and mechanics;

o improving literacy and numeracy skills;

o health education;

o seeking and maintaining employment; and

o looking at ways to break the routine of offending

Detailed below is Kent's START programme as outlined in its *Guide for Sentencers and Probation Officers*:

The START course – cognitive skills
START = straight talking and reasoned thinking
This course is at the core of the Probation Centre Programme. It has been developed under the title 'Reasoning and Rehabilitation' by Professor Robert Ross and his colleagues at the University of Ottowa and is now in use in rehabilitation centres – both prisons and community based – in different parts of the world.

The sessions focus on modifying the impulsive, egocentric, illogical and rigid thinking of some offenders. The goal is to teach them to stop and think before acting, consider the consequences of their behaviour, conceptualise alternative ways of responding to inter-personal problems and consider the impact of their behaviour on other people (including their victims). There is a process of repetition and reinforcement built into the programme to facilitate this.

This programme is probably the most highly developed and researched ever produced for use with offenders and as results are coming through they are distinctly encouraging its effectiveness.

Offenders will work through nine inter-related modules:

o Problem solving   o Values enhancement
o Social skills   o Critical reasoning
o Negotiation skills   o Skills in review
o Management of emotion   o Cognitive exercises
o Creative thinking

The programme has been used with a wide range of offenders and is particularly suited to the more seriously convicted individuals with which Probation Centres deal. One difference from other programmes is the systematic building-block approach which requires probationers to be part of a stable group throughout the course.

To complement the START sessions, probationers have access to a well-equipped craft/carpentry workshop and garage in which they can develop practical skills. Tutors provide sessions in art, basic education (literacy and numeracy) and health education. For those who are unemployed, 'job search' is a compulsory element and all probationers are supported by personal interviews with their supervising probation officer.

In addition to the basic programme, special projects are mounted periodically.

Educational outings, outward-bound activities, Duke of Edinburgh Awards, art and drama therapy, sports competitions, burglar/victim mediation and motor mechanics are examples of work done in the Probation Centre over past years.

Whilst at the Centres probationers may be eligible to gain a Vocational Access Certificate which can be used – with an employer or a training advisor for example – to provide evidence of personal development.

Whilst a concentration is always maintained on reducing offending it is recognised that a constructive approach to individuals is essential to maintain their interest and co-operation. There are indeed many ways in which offenders can be encouraged to develop and to behave better.

The programme attempts to respond to the various reasons for offending. It also attempts to maintain the interest and active participation of all involved by balancing work on confronting offending behaviour with educational activities, development of social skills and health sessions.

There is an emphasis on working together and valuing the role of everyone in the Centre. The individual skills of staff members are fully utilised. Administrative staff are happy to teach typing and probation officers are as likely to be found in the workshop as in an offending behaviour group. Lunchtime and other periods are set aside for informal contact.

The work at the Centre complements the normal requirements of a probation order. The same probation officer is responsible for both the order and the work at the Centre although this can be negotiated if there are extenuating circumstances.

Each person attending the Centre is asked to sign a contract before the programme commences.

Sample contract
1. I agree to attend Medway Probation Day Centre for 60 days as directed by the Probation Officer in charge of the Day Centre.
2. I agree to arrive on time on the days I have to attend. If I am ill or there is a good reason for me not to come in, I will make sure that the staff are informed on the same day. I understand that any illnesses must be covered by a medical certificate and must cover the days I am absent. In the cases of prolonged illness, I will ensure that the

medical certificates are forwarded to the Probation Day Centre at the earliest opportunity.

3. I agree to take part in all the aspects of the programme at Medway probation Day Centre, or connected with it.

4. I agree not to engage in any violent, threatening, disruptive or dishonest behaviour whilst attending the Medway Probation Day Centre or taking part in any activity connected with the Day Centre.

5. I agree that I will not bring any alcohol, unprescribed drugs or solvents (e.g., glue) into the Centre. I will not take any of these things while I am at the Centre or involved in any activity undertaken in connection with the Day Centre, nor attend under their influence.

6. I agree that if I use a motor vehicle to travel to Medway Probation Day Centre I will show staff a driving licence, insurance and other related documents. I agree not to park illegally or as a nuisance to others. I understand that I cannot use my own vehicle for travel on Medway Probation Day Centre activities.

7. I agree to attend the evening programme as directed should I obtain work. Should I lose my job, I agree to return to the day programme.

8. I understand that failure to comply with any part of this contract could lead me to being returned to court for breach of the Probation Order.

Results

There has been a positive response by those who have attended the Centre. Some of their comments could apply to any of the schemes discussed in this book:

'I got into trouble because of money problems and to feel grown up with all the older lads.'

'It helps me learn before it's too late.'

'The project is helping me find out things, looking for a job and helping me stay out of trouble.'

'The project is very helpful to me and there should be more

choices for other people.'

'Coming here during the day helps me stay out of trouble.'

'I started getting into trouble for greed and personal gain'.

'If I go to prison, I think it will be a never-ending cycle.'

'This project makes me think and it's harder than going inside!'

Chapter 7

Motor Projects

Background: National Association of Motor Projects

National Association of Motor Projects, c/o John Clarke,
14 Chetwode Road, Tadworth , Surrey , KT20 5PW
Telephone: Tadworth (07373) 52567

Car related offences are amongst the most common to come
before the courts and are a particular feature of juvenile and
young offending. The table below, supplied by the statistics
division of the Prison Service, demonstrates, over a five-month
period in early 1993,

a) the number of sentenced juveniles in prison custody
b) the number of unsentenced juveniles in prison custody
c) the number of sentenced juveniles convicted of car crimes
d) the percentage of juveniles convicted of car crimes
   compared to the overall juvenile population.

Date	Total no. of sentenced juveniles	Total no. of unsentenced juveniles	No. convicted for car crimes	%
26 February 1993	701	127	100	14.0
26 March 1993	750	139	145	19.0
30 April 1993	741	129	130	17.5
28 May 1993	802	110	137	17.0
18 June 1993	781	115	121	15.5

During the summer of 1991, the events on Oxford's Blackbird
Leys and Newcastle's Meadowell Estates generated massive
media attention and provoked a swift government response.
Increased penalties were announced and £5 million set
aside for a publicity campaign.

The dangers of offences like joy-riding are obvious. Teenagers
will usually be inexperienced drivers incapable of coping with

unexpected situations. Death or serious injury can result, in addition to the usual insurance and other costs to the victim. However, it is clear that increasing penalties and car security does little to address the causes of this type of offending.

In 1986, the National Association of Motor Projects was formed to promote educational and vocational training for those under 25 who are at risk of offending or re-offending. There are approximately seventy member projects and each can approach their task in a different way.

Major differences in the solutions each project employs will depend on how the project is viewed locally and, crucially, by the availability of funding and resources. Local Authority Youth Service provision or Home Office Safer Cities funding might allow for more preventative or diversionary work. Funding associated with the Probation Service will require work with older and convicted young people.

A popular conception of the motor project is that of the 'banger project': an Intermediate Treatment project where a 'charismatic mechanic' holds sway and where 'boys will be boys', including the workers and volunteers. Such projects may still exist and many of those involved in all projects will admit to an ongoing passion for cars. However, many projects are now addressing the wider social issues and the very real need to satisfy funders and the courts that motor projects work.

The Home Office's research into joy-riding and car crime (Light *et al*; Webb and Laycock) emphasises that the initial reasons for car theft are excitement and peer pressure. Different conclusions can be drawn from this.

One school of thought holds that because car theft is so exciting, only something which is just as exciting, such as banger racing or karting, can grab the interest of the (mostly) young men doing it. An opposing view is that nothing, not even drugs or sex, can match the excitement of car theft. This second school points to the experience of Belfast where the prospect of alleged kneecapping by the IRA or shooting by the security forces at road blocks fails to deter joy-riding. This can lead to a 'nothing works' conclusion.

Experience suggests that some projects do work but research

is limited and often carried out by the projects themselves.

What is clear is that sanctions such as disqualification or imprisonment are of limited value with young people. The Telford Drive for Shropshire Project suggests the following reasons for this:

1. the younger the age at which the offending starts, the less able young people are to appreciate the enormity of their actions;
2. the length of time represented by periods of disqualification is beyond the experience span of these young people. It asks the individual to wait a period of time which seems too long for him/her to comprehend maturely;
3. disqualification confirms and heightens the status of an individual as an illegal driver and, accordingly, adds to his/her offending image;
4. disqualification does nothing to satiate the need and/or desire to drive;
5. whilst sanctioning, taking away the opportunity to drive legally does nothing to engage the offender constructively in issues surrounding legal driving aimed at improving attitudes and offending behaviour;
6. disqualification ensures that any further offending of a like kind will result in an increase in the severity of the offence.

Young people involved in the Telford Project who have spent time in prison are also clear about the ineffectiveness of custody:

John, who initially went to prison for a non-car-related offence.

Q. What did prison do for you?
A. It taught me to pinch cars, take alarms off and all that.
Q. Did you know much about taking cars before you went to prison?
A. I didn't know a lot ... not much at all.
Q. And when you came out?
A. It was just easy. The first one might have been a bit hard ... but after that, it just came easy.

Q. So really, you'd recommend prison to people who want to take cars.

A. Yeah, you're damn right.

Steve

Q. Did prison put you off stealing cars?

A. No, it made me worse. I was nicking just 125s before I went away but when I came out I was nicking high performance cars and bikes ... When I came out the first time, I re-offended within 3–4 days.

Q. What happened the last time?

A. I was given probation with a condition of compulsory attendance at a motor group. We did things like discuss the victims and what it causes them and the insurance ... the police and probation were also involved ... before that, I used to take cars 3–4 times a week or even daily. . . Locking up doesn't help at all.

Here, we look at some projects which operate in different areas, have different funding arrangements and use cars differently:

Bradford Motor Education Project

Bradford Motor Education Project, PO Box 6, City Courts, Bradford, West Yorkshire BD1 1LB
Telephone: Bradford (0274) 680508

This project initially formed part of an alternative to custody scheme which operated between 1984 and 1987. After this funding ended, officers from Youth Services and Probation formed a steering committee which was eventually able to secure funding for the project as a crime prevention scheme in 1991 with money from Safer Cities.

A further grant from the Home Office Probation Service Division's Supervision Grant Scheme (then the Young Adult Offender Grant Scheme) in 1992 allowed the project to add its Crime Challenge Unit. This takes offenders as a condition of a probation order and offers a planned suite of sessions in motor mechanics with the local community college, group work with the Probation Service on victims, road safety and health issues as well as one-to-one work on issues identified by the Probation Service. There is also a women's only group led by women mechanics.

The Project works with about 400 people on a number of estates with high car crime rates using karts, bangers, mini-stox, motor bikes and a hovercraft.

Results

During the first six months of operation on the Holmewood Estate, one of the largest in Europe, there was a 2% reduction in auto crime at a time when there was a 40% national increase.

The Bradford Motor Education Project's Annual Report for the year ending 31 March 1993 provides the following breakdown:

Statistical return 1992/93

Total referrals received 79
Referral status: Seeking probation order 78
Seeking parole condition 1

Ethnicity of referrals:
White European 71
Asian 5
Afro Caribbean 2
Other 1

Gender of referrals:
Male 78
Female 1

Age of referrals:

Age:	16	17	18	19	20	21	22	23	24	25	25+
Number:	1	8	4	15	6	10	10	6	2	3	14

Status at referral:
Bail 55
Custody 24

Referral take-up by Project:
Accepted   64
Refused   15

Reasons for refusal

Over age	4
Custody for other offences prior to assessment	2
Unsuitable by attitude/addictions	5
Withdrawn by probation officer following consultation	4

Take-up by courts of accepted referrals

BMEP condition order made by court	42
BMEP condition imposed by parole board	1
Pending court decision	3
BMEP conditions rejected by court	18

The Report concludes:

The project has been successful in attracting a wide range of referrals and of these, 81% were deemed appropriate for acceptance. Of the referrals accepted, we were able to obtain orders in 70% of cases. This led to the project being over-subscribed in terms of its 40 allocated places.

There is considerable enthusiasm for the project amongst both probation offices and the courts and this has been sustained by the progress made by offenders coming on to the Project.

To date, only 16% of orders have been terminated for further offences or breach of order. The effectiveness of the Project has led to the Probation Service seeking to extend the scope of the Project across the probation area to provide equality of service. This extension was approved by the Home Office for the financial years 93/94 and 94/95.

Ilderton Motor Project, South London

Ilderton Motor Project, 80a Edward Street, London SE8 5HB
Telelephone: 081 469 0396

'Ilderton has always concentrated on the positive approach. We recognise that joy-riding is hazardous to the public but we also know

that it is equally hazardous to the children and young people who steal and drive cars with little or no ability or sense of responsibility. They have never learnt that the car is potentially a lethal weapon. All they have gleaned about cars has come from TV and films, glossy magazines and aggressive advertising.

'They have absorbed the seductive "macho" message and they want some of the action without appreciating the consequences. They feel, often for the first time in their lives, really alive, "empowered" behind the wheel of a desirable car. They obtain a ready-made sense of identity and a rush of adrenalin. They need to drive – and they need help.

'After years of interviewing and working with joy-riders, we know that the majority are neither malicious thugs nor killers. They are little more than children playing with dangerous toys under the illusion that they are invulnerable. When accidents do happen, the joy-riders are frequently as devastated by the results as the innocent people who suffer as a result.

'It is all too easy to support the knee-jerk "hang 'em and flog 'em" response. Unwittingly, however, this only serves to compound the problem. Joy-riding is anti-social but the response to it has to be positive'.

Peter West, Project leader

This project has been operating since 1976 and is probably the best known of its kind.

Ilderton only takes 20 young people at a time, mostly as a condition of a probation order or voluntarily with another order such as community service.

It is funded by Inner London Probation Service and Lewisham Council so can also take self-referrals. However, the limited workshop space means there is a waiting list for official and self-referrals. Young women have also undertaken work at the project although, at present, there are no female staff or volunteers to allow this.

The workshop is the centre of activity on four evenings a week, including one compulsory evening for those on orders. At these sessions, bangers are prepared for racing at commercial stadia. Volunteers provide informal social work during these sessions with formal sessions being held each Wednesday

173

evening. These meetings provide staff and those attending with an opportunity to resolve personal and group problems.

Craig's Story

'One of the first times I started to get into trouble was when I first went to my secondary school. I arrived three weeks late and almost immediately I started to get picked on, because everyone had already met each other and I was the odd one out.

I tried my hardest to keep out of trouble but in the end it caught up with me and I started having lots of fights.

After a while, I was seen as the bad one, and eventually got expelled. Then I met up with a group of boys and that's when I started to get in deep. Like, one day I got a lift home – in a stolen car. Then eventually I stole a car myself and drove it to near my house.

I think I did it because there was nothing for all of us to do. Youth clubs and things like that had all been closed down.

A little later I got pinched by the police and ended up in prison for six weeks. That's where I learnt all about stealing better cars. That's all people talked about, so you got to know a lot.

When I came out, I was out of work. By this time, I had bricklaying skills, but still couldn't find any work. I had children, so I started stealing cars because they were so easy to nick.

It was such easy money that it was too hard to refuse.

After a couple of years, I'd had nearly every punishment you can have, but it all got nowhere. They put me on probation and community service but nothing helped me until I got sent to the Ilderton Motor Project.

I am not saying that I stopped as soon I got through the door, but something I got from them was respect and a lot of responsibility from the staff.

After a short time, I could see what they could do for me, so I worked at it because I knew it could help me.

And it did. Three and a half years later, I am now a voluntary member of staff. I had to show them I was capable of doing the job, like going to conferences all over the place and talking to loads of people – police officers, magistrates, students and reporters about the Project. I've got a lot of responsibility now in helping out on the Project.

And I help to get other projects going. One day I might be able to get a proper job with the Probation Service as I like helping young kids. I really get a lot of pleasure out of helping them.'

Lee's Story

'I first became involved in crime when I moved to Charlton (south London). At first my dad was working but he became unemployed and had to go on the social security which meant I didn't get any pocket money.

Then I met a bunch of kids and started to hang about with them. We used to get bored so we started stealing from cars. One day, we tried to steal from a Honda Civic. We tried to roll the car downhill but it had four flat tyres. As the car began to roll, the police came up the hill and nicked me and my friend. They took us down to the station and rang my mum and dad. My dad came and picked me up. I had to go back six weeks later to find out what was going to happen. When I did go back, they said I had to go to court.

When I went to court, the judge said I had to pay £7.50. I had to see a social worker and she asked me what I wanted to do with my life. I told her I liked cars. She asked me if I wanted to go the Ilderton Motor Project and I said yes.

I went for an interview with Pete West, the project leader, and he said I could start in two weeks. So I started the Project, and was shown around and met all the other members of the Project.

At the Project, I learned how to drive and I know a lot about cars now. I have had three races. I think the Project is a good place and I have never been in trouble since I started there.

Every Wednesday, we have a meeting and talk about the Project, and anything else that is worrying us in our lives. The Project is the best thing that has happened in my life.'

Despite the small numbers involved and the apparent simplicity of its methods, Ilderton is in the forefront of publicising motor projects and of innovative thinking about ways of tackling car crime. For example, it has made a video and developed a drama workshop on joy-riding with a local community theatre group, Theatre Adad.

Results

The last formal research into Ilderton was undertaken in 1980. That showed that 70% of the 144 young people who had passed through the Project over the preceding three years had not offended while members of the Project. Future research is planned but these figures remain important when put in the following context:

- 80% of offenders re-offend in the first of release from prison custody;
- custodial places cost £400 upwards per week per prisoner;
- a place on the Ilderton Motor Project costs £30 per week.

Theatre Adad

Theatre Adad, PO Box 3551, London SE14 5PU
Telephone: 0753 573846

With the help of Ilderton, Theatre Adad has developed a twenty-minute drama for primary schools. The theatre brings out the excitement and dangers of car crime and is followed by a discussion, role-play and creative workshops which give children the chance to think how they might say 'no'. It also gives them the chance to compose a slogan, rap or poem against car crime – for example, '*Stop you fool, it's not very cool.*'

Since October 1992, Theatre Adad has performed in schools in Deptford, Wandsworth and Middlesborough and before an older youth audience in Stevenage. The work in Wandsworth schools is currently being evaluated by Wandsworth Safer Cities.

Kent Auto Offenders Scheme

58 College Road, Maidstone, Kent, ME15 6SJ
Telephone: Maidstone (0622) 750934

Background
'*The attitude is often that they reckon if someone has a car, that means they can afford it and they also convince themselves that it's probably insured anyway so it doesn't matter if they take it.*

'*But what stops them is when you start to develop their concern and care for others.*

'*You have to show them that someone might lose their job because their car is stolen, that someone might have to get someone to hospital in a hurry and can't because their car has been stolen. That people get injured and killed after being involved with people who are joy-riding.*

'It's the element of care and concern that is important – the financial side does not encourage them to identify with the loser at all'.

Kent Probation Officer

Dick Whitfield, Chief Probation Officer at Kent Probation, describes how the auto offenders' scheme was instigated.

The level of car crime in Kent had been going up consistently over the last five years and we had known for some time that there were young offenders on our books whose behaviour verged on the obsessional – which for the unfortunate motorist frequently meant they were stealing two or three cars a night. More and more punishment with longer and longer disqualifications was, however, simply producing another set of problems and it was decided that a different kind of answer was needed. After a bit of early experiment, what emerged was a special course as part of a Probation Order run over 10 weeks. Unusually the course is not run just by the Probation Service but as a partnership affair with the Kent Police and the Kent Ambulance Service.

Over a ten-week period youngsters on the Auto Offenders Group do some intensive work on: offending patterns and what they mean, motorists and the law, basic mechanics, responsible driving, first aid and a range of other topics related to their own experience.

The police input is specifically targeted at their own patterns of behaviour and the ambulance service show some very graphic videos on the results of irresponsible driving as well as practical help which can be given at the scene of an accident. It is a sobering, demanding and interesting 10 weeks and it finishes with a full day spent at Brands Hatch with Early Drive Ltd who use the urban driving area to concentrate on responsible driving techniques.

This is not the only Auto Offenders Group in the country, of course, but what has been remarkable is the level of success it has achieved and of the first fifty young people who went through it in a two-year follow up only six had reoffended. The results have been so impressive that the course has been extended to cover all courts in Kent and it has also been very influential in shaping Auto Offender Courses elsewhere. It has achieved recognition (of a sort) from sources as diverse as the *Daily Telegraph*, Michael Jack MP and a local television station and in some ways it has helped to reshape attitudes to a crucial group of young offenders who won't go away.

The last and most important point I think is that the course does not end with the 10 week intensive group. The Probation Officers involved concentrate thereafter on sensible ban management so that the young offenders do not lose the momentum they have gained. This is included in applications to courts for periods of disqualification to be reduced mediation with Insurance Companies and generally reinforcing the notion that driving legally is a sensible and realisable goal.'

Dick Whitfield, Chief Probation Officer

Stuart's Story

'I first went joy-riding with a friend when I was 18. I didn't feel any sympathy for the owner but we did make sure we didn't damage the car before we dumped it several miles away.

'I passed my driver's test when I was 18 and got my first car. Back then, I was a real boy-racer. I loved speeding because it was exciting – but I soon ended up with a fine. I was out of work at the time, so I decided to steal a couple of things like car radios which were easy to sell.

'I hadn't been in trouble with the police before so I thought I'd get away with it. I wouldn't get caught. Looking back on it, I think I behaved like a prat.

'The real trouble started when someone stole my car. I'd scrimped and saved to buy it and someone stole it from a car park and smashed it up. I couldn't believe it.

'Then a couple of us went out one night and saw this car parked in the street. I suppose I was bitter that my car had been taken, so we decided to take it.

'The police knocked at my door two weeks later. My parents were shocked and angry. But I was 18. I thought I could go out when I liked, go the pub and get drunk. I do feel bad about what I put my parents through and for making them feel ashamed.

'The first court appearance was nerve-racking and I was banned from driving for nine months and given a hefty fine. I got a job in London to clear the fine, and was able to buy another car and get back on the road after my ban had ended.

'I continued to get into trouble with the police for things like speeding. Then I decided to steal the number plates off someone else's car, put them on my own, fill up with petrol and drive off without paying. But the local CID saw me removing the plates and followed me. There was a chase and I was eventually surrounded by five police cars.

'At the court hearing, the probation officer recommended going on to the Auto Project. I didn't really know what to expect from the course. I thought it would be a bit of a skive. But it isn't and I think that instead of banging people away, the courts should send them on projects like this.

'I swear that since I've been on it, I can guarantee you that I will never steal another car or go joy-riding again.

'We were shown pictures of babies that had been injured, people without limbs and someone's head that had been severed in a crash. An ambulance worker also showed us a film of people being cut out of cars in terrible pain.

'The crimes I committed were never planned. It's an ego boost for some people. They like to steal a flashy car and show off to the girls walking down the street. They think it makes you a man.

'I've done it and I've learnt from it. I can see the attraction but it's not worth it. Insurance for my age would have cost me £450 but because of my ban I have to pay £900.

'I feel ashamed of my past and ashamed of what I put my family through. I didn't realise what might have happened until I came on this course.'

Results

The scheme was established in a year when thefts of vehicles in Kent rose by nearly 30%. However, over a two-year follow-up period, only 6 of the first 50 young people who completed the course have re-offended.

These impressive results have led to the course being extended to cover all courts in Kent and to similar auto offending projects being developed elsewhere.

Chapter 8

Partnerships

The emphasis on community sentences in the Criminal Justice Act 1991 makes liaison between all those involved in the criminal justice process increasingly important.

As a Home Office letter to Chief Probation Officers and Justices' Clerks pointed out, ' . . . in the new area of pre-sentence reports and the new range of community sentences, it is essential for Magistrates' Courts and the Probation Service to develop a common understanding.' (CPO 84\1992 Probation Service Liaison with Sentencers, 21 December 1992)

Local Authority Circular LAC 92(5) also emphasises a joint approach to the provision of services to the Youth Court.

The idea of partnerships became firmly established amongst criminal justice practitioners during the 1980s. The two main features of this trend have been the creation of specialist, inter-agency youth justice teams and the involvement of the voluntary sector in the creation or ongoing operation of these units.

Inter-agency teams

The Diversion Unit,

198 Kettering Road, Northampton NN1 4BL
Telephone: Northampton (0604) 601241

Exeter Youth Justice Scheme

1 Higher Summerlands, Exeter EX1 2LW
Telephone: Exeter (0392) 50327

In both Northampton and Exeter, specialist agencies were created following joint initiatives from the police, the Probation Service and Social Services. In both cases, the chief constable played a leading role in establishing the partnership and the both schemes served as models for other counties including

Kent, Surrey and Hampshire.

The juvenile justice units which were created review the cases of all juveniles who enter the criminal justice system and are responsible for implementing community sentences and other support.

This approach succeeds best when there are clear and agreed principles of intervention such as those underpinning the work in Northampton:

Principles of intervention

1) the reason for intervention should be clear, explicit and have positive consequences for the offender or injured party;
2) intervention should be directed towards resolving the offence informally and treating the offender as a normal adolescent;
3) minimum intervention should be used;
4) intervention should increase the amount of community involvement and create a greater tolerance and understanding of juvenile crime;
5) concern should be shown for the injured party as well as for the offender.

Intervention takes place for the following reasons:

1) serious or persistent offences have been committed;
2) there appear to be related problems in the family/school/ community;
3) there is apparent concern within the community about particular or recurrent types of offence;
4) there is apparent failure of the community or agencies to respond to the problems of juvenile crime informally, in positive and constructive ways;
5) there is a positive outcome to be gained for the offender and the injured party by addressing compensation, reparation or apology.

The Exeter team has identified further advantages in this method of work:

- a single, co-ordinated response to youth crime has been developed;
- an atmosphere of trust, co-operation and professional respect has developed. This has given confidence to those developing non-custodial alternatives for those under 17;
- the experience of these three agencies (police, probation and social services) working together has been a catalyst for the involvement of other agencies in the management of youth crime;
- the creation of the Youth Support Team has enabled a wider focus on young offending e.g., crime prevention and direct work within schools.

Partnership arrangements with the voluntary sector
The voluntary sector has become involved in youth justice work in a variety of ways and now receives government funding to provide non-custodial alternatives for young people.

Hampshire, Kent and Durham provide three of the earliest examples of this involvement.

Hampshire Juvenile Justice Service

North Hants Juvenile Justice Unit, Woodlands Centre,
180 Culver Road, Basingstoke, RG21 3NL
Telephone: Basingstoke (0256) 464034/20766

South East Hants Juvenile Justice Unit

Darby House, Southwick Hill Road, Cosham,
Portsmouth PO6 3LU
Telephone: Portsmouth (0705) 370013

South West Hants Juvenile Justice Unit

33 Selborne Avenue, Harefield, Southampton SO2 5DZ
Telephone: Southampton (0703) 463336

Background
In 1980, a Basingstoke magistrate initiated contact with the Rainer Foundation with the aim of establishing a project which

could offer an alternative to custody for serious juvenile offenders.

As a result, the 'Woodlands Project' was established in 1981 and provided intermediate treatment for juveniles as a requirement of a supervision order. It was one of the first examples of a scheme jointly involving the Social Services and a national charity. It quickly acquired a reputation for being guided and supported by the Basingstoke Justices' Clerk and magistrates.

Management was assisted by a local advisory group, initially chaired by the magistrate, and involving representatives from the Probation Service, Social Services and the police.

Because of the way it developed, the Woodlands Project had an immediate impact in the courts. This created a problem with inappropriate referrals comprising some young people whose offences where not serious or persistent enough to warrant intrusive intervention. Between 1981 and 1983, twenty of the fifty young people referred for assessment were rejected by the Woodlands staff. None of the twenty subsequently received a custodial sentence or a Woodlands programme.

However, the Woodlands project did succeed in reducing the use of custody for young people. Basingstoke magistrates imposed 18 custodial sentences in 1980. This fell to 5 in 1982 and 3 in 1983.

Further Developments

Services for juvenile offenders in the Hampshire area were generally extended during the period 1981–1986.

In 1983, the Department of Health released £15 million nationally to the voluntary sector for the development of alternative, non-custodial projects for young offenders and young people at risk of offending (intermediate treatment programmes).

In 1987, the Hampshire Juvenile Justice Service was established. Again, the involvement of magistrates and justices' clerks was crucial. The chairs of Juvenile Courts were consulted and direct representation was made to the Probation and Social Services committees. Those involved in the consultation process describe it as hard work but acknowledge it was undertaken in an atmosphere of goodwill and co-operation.

John Harding, the Chief Probation Officer at the time, stressed the importance of a service with a 'strong political ownership', i.e., one which the chairs of juvenile panels and magistrates' committees are more likely to support because they have helped shape and develop it.

Overall management of the Juvenile Justice Service is therefore in the hands of a prominent committee which represents all the parties involved.

Both the chief officers of the Probation Service and Social Services are keen to work effectively together. Magistrates, police, solicitors and members of the Crown Prosecution Service regularly attend open days and joint training sessions.

The Juvenile Justice Service built on the work of the Woodlands Project and other intermediate treatment schemes in Southampton and Portsmouth. Four specialist units were established based on the existing intermediate treatment centres. The Woodlands scheme developed into the Basingstoke Youth Justice Team which adopted the same aims and operational principles.

Each of the four units was given responsibility for the following:

- screening of police referrals for prosecution to aid in diversion of young offenders from the criminal justice system, through regular meetings with the police and other agencies to provide an opportunity to suggest diversion from court in appropriate cases which have not been instantly cautioned;
- the preparation of social enquiry reports (replaced with pre-sentence reports under the 1991 Criminal Justice Act);
- the supervision of young persons subject to supervision orders for criminal offences;
- the supervision of those subject to community service orders up to the age of 17 years (the Criminal Justice Act 1991 extended this to include people up to 18 years old);
- those young offenders who are the subject of post-custody care;

- ○ the provision of credible programmes for serious and persistent offenders as a direct alternative to custody and care orders.

Kent Youth Justice Service

c/o Development Officer, Residential Services, 123 High Street, West Malling, Kent ME19 6NE
Telephone: West Malling (0703) 870987
NB: There are a number of other units throughout Kent

Background

Kent provides an example of joint work involving the charity, Community Volunteer Service (CVS).

Eight Juvenile Justice Teams were established in Kent following the allocation to CVS of £326,000 per year for four years from the 1983 Department of Health intermediate treatment grants.

The teams were set up to provide the juvenile courts with non-custodial programmes on behalf of the local authority. Each scheme consisted of staff appointed by CVS and chosen for their ability to work with young people in trouble, rather than for their social work qualifications.

Each team was managed by the Social Services Intermediate Treatment Officer who reported to an inter-agency management group consisting of representatives from the local magistrates, Social Services, Probation, the police and the Education Service.

This local group was responsible for the development of local inter-agency co-operation and practice.

The inter-agency groups reported to a county reference group consisting of senior managers from all the agencies. This reference group advised the County Chief Officers Group which had overall responsibility for formulating policy in relation to young offenders.

In 1987, CVS helped consolidate a joint service for young offenders. The agencies involved produced a combined report, *A Strategy for the Developing of Inter-Agency Services for Juvenile*

Offenders, Juvenile Crime and Juvenile Justice in Kent – Report of the Inter-Agency Working Group, 1987, which recommended the establishment of a Joint Juvenile Justice Service.

It also formulated the common aims for the agencies involved:

○ prevention of juvenile offending;
○ diversion from the Juvenile Court;
○ development of community-based programmes for those offenders at risk of care or custody;
○ reduction in the numbers receiving custody.

Kent provides an example of a large Social Services Department in which responsibility for the development of inter-agency services for young offenders is delegated to middle managers with a serious commitment to fighting for their projects. Peter Gilroy, the Senior Assistant Director of Social Services, describes them as 'champions for the cause . . . keeping the mantel of services for young offenders alive alongside the other priorities we face'. Without this commitment, many non-custodial projects would not have got off the ground.

Further Developments

The CVS initiatives also led to the formation of five Juvenile Offender Liaison Teams (JOLT) in Kent consisting of staff seconded from the police, Social Services, the Education Department and the Probation Service.

The seconded police officer represents the JOLT team in negotiations with senior police officers over cautioning and diversion.

The experience has been that this arrangement only works if the seconded officer is prepared to accept being managed by an officer employed by a different agency and enjoys working alongside colleagues with different conditions of service.

However, seconded officers see the advantage of the arrangement being a much greater understanding within the services of the role of the police and an acceptance within the police of the value of the JOLT teams.

Results

CVS made a significant impact during the four years of intermediate treatment funding. The custody rate for young people
dropped from 14.6% in 1983 to 5.9% in 1986. The number of
young people appearing before the Juvenile Court dropped by
46%.

Having one team responsible for all the Youth Court services
makes the collection of data much easier to co-ordinate, and
effectiveness more simple to monitor. The Service produces
comprehensive figures every six months and a joint police/
social services data base is planned.

Figures for period 1 January 1992 to 30 June 1992 show that:

o the cases of 428 young people were referred to JOLT;
o 217 cases (50.7%) were diverted by the JOLT team from
  prosecution;
o 85 of the 211 (40.3%) who appeared before court had at
  least one previous conviction and 27 (12.8%) had three or
  more previous court appearances;
o 83.9% of the 211 prosecuted cases were from the older
  male group (14–17).
o 8.5% were female, none of whom were from the 10–13 age
  group;
o 413 (96.5%) were of white ethnic origin;
o 10 custodial sentences were imposed, 7 of which were for
  offences against property;
o 28.9% were dealt with by conditional discharge, the most
  commonly imposed sentence;
o 28 cases (13.5%) were withdrawn by the CPS after reaching
  the Juvenile Court;
o in 92 cases (67.1%), the final sentence matched the
  recommendation in the Social Inquiry Report.

The Contract Project, County Durham

4th Floor, Cathedral Buildings, 29 Dean Street,
Newcastle NE1 1PG
Telephone: Newcastle (091) 232 3258

This project was established in 1984 as part of the expansion of the Hilltop Project in West Yorkshire. The Durham Youth Development Project arranged with the Save the Children Fund, who had developed Hilltop in 1980 to provide training and consultancy services for the development of intermediate treatment programmes, to provide training and assistance. Contract became a separate Save the Children Fund Project with Intermediate Treatment funding.

Further Developments
Contract went on to play a more general role developing non-custodial alternatives for young people. In particular, the County Youth Development Trust commissioned Contract to evaluate the work of six non-custodial projects within the County.

The subsequent evaluation reports led to expanded funding for non-custodial projects and, over the next three years, Contract set up and serviced two inter-agency practice development groups involving Social Services, Probation and the police. These formed the basis of two specialist teams of juvenile justice workers.

A further by-product was the creation of the Young Offenders Resource Unit in January 1990. This incorporated the functions of existing projects in the area under one management structure and aimed to put responsibility for work with young offenders into the hands of a single body. It provides an example of the kind of creative inter-agency practice that can be developed if change takes place in a planned and co-ordinated way within all levels of the system.

By October 1992, this unit had enabled the youth justice team in the south of the county to expand its programmes. They now provide programmes for supervision orders with additional requirements, a remand foster scheme and a bail support scheme. Their crime prevention work includes a schools' crime prevention project and work with local youth development groups.

Contract has also been active in other areas. In 1988, in partnership with the Probation Service, it became involved with a social action and community development group on estates in Peterlee. A development worker was appointed to work with local young people and has successfully engaged them in helping plan improvements to home security and living conditions.

Contract also provides training programmes for youth justice, probation and education staff. For example, Cleveland Probation Service uses Contract in its core training programmes for officers working with offenders.

Contract also provides training and development on information and evaluation systems and has appointed a development officer to assist other agencies in the design and use of information systems and the analysis of criminal justice data.

Case Study: Darren

When Darren attended court in April 1988, he expected a custodial sentence to be the eventual outcome. His father requested a custodial sentence for his son, believing that custody would teach Darren a lesson. He had served a number of custodial sentences in his youth himself and eventually 'learned his lesson'. Despite his father's request, the magistrate decided to adjourn Darren's case for a period of three weeks while Springboard assessed his suitability for a programme.

Initially the assessment progressed well despite the negative attitude shown by Darren's father. Darren was punctual at all appointments, guarded in his response to his outreach worker, but expressing a desire to avoid further offending. Unfortunately, during the second week of his assessment, the relationship between Darren and his father became very strained. Darren entered his father's bedroom without permission and this resulted in an explosive argument. Darren ran away from home. Close consultation between Darren's father, supervising officer and Springboard followed. His father agreed that, could Darren be found, it would be wise for him to be taken into voluntary care.

This would allow both Darren and his father breathing space.

Darren was eventually found, told of the plans and agreed to go to a small local authority home. Within two days of admission, problems arose as a result of peers wishing to establish leadership. There was a fight in which Darren received a number of minor injuries. He felt that life was hopeless, rejected by his father (his mother had left home when he was 3 years old), rejected by his peers, he talked quite seriously about suicide.

Despite Darren's belief that he had been rejected by everyone, Springboard worked hard with him to try and convince him that he was important and that people did care. Slowly, he began to respond. He was directed to attend Springboard for 4 months following his assessment. During his first group session, he told other group members that his ambition was to become a professional cat burglar.

Gradually, his life began to settle down. Although his relationship with his father improved, his dad did not want him to return home. Action had to be taken to find a more suitable and permanent situation for Darren. He progressed into a more permanent unit in the children's home and was admitted into a local comprehensive school. It was the first time he had attended school in over a year. Staff at the school soon recognised that Darren was a bright, talented child who needed a great deal of support and encouragement.

Work continued, challenging Darren's attitude towards offending, helping him recognise the effect his actions had upon his victims, his father and subsequently himself. His attitude began to change, he began to realise he didn't need to offend in order to gain recognition. He left Springboard, having enroled for GCSE exams, displaying talent as an artist and with a positive approach to his future.

Springboard Alternative to Custody Project, 1988

Darren's case illustrates problems faced by many young people involved in offending. The experience of the Springboard Project and others like it throughout the country is that care and attention to particular problems can help young people move away from criminal behaviour.

In previous chapters, we have looked at specific sentencing alternatives to custody, many of which, while also providing alternatives to local care, mirror Durham's experience.

Results

The changes initiated by Contract in Durham had a significant impact. Between 1986 and 1989, the number of juveniles annually sentenced to care or custody fell by 90% from 189 to 18. During the same period, changes in police cautioning policy and the establishment of juvenile liaison panels led to a 30% drop in prosecutions from 1,439 to 1,011.

The Young Offenders Resource Unit 1992 Annual Report concludes:

> There have been a number of indications that the young people we are working with are facing more severe problems than in the past . . . (leading to) a greater danger of re-offending . . .

> . . . there has been an increase in the frequency of offending for young people prior to them being assigned to alternative to custody programmes . . . highlighting the increased seriousness of the offenders we deal with. With regard to the effects on young people's behaviour we believe we are maintaining our position as a viable alternative to custody and as a provider of effective community sentence programmes and support packages . . .

The growing importance of the voluntary sector

The team leader of the Durham Young Offenders' Resource Unit states that the involvement of the Save the Children Fund as a voluntary agency has 'helped us stop being ingrained in statutory type practice'.

While the government has its own reasons for promoting the voluntary sector above local authorities and welfare agencies, this experience highlights the increasing importance of the voluntary sector which, in March 1992, was allocated £10 million under the Probation Supervision Grants Scheme for non-residential probation projects.

In some cases, the voluntary sector has played a key role in the development of schemes for young offenders. In others, it has been more of an 'honest broker' between the major agencies. Either way, it has helped shift the focus away from purely institutional responses to young offending over the past ten years and is gaining increasing respect from judges and magistrates.

Throughout the country, the costs and benefits of partnership agreements have been similar.

Benefits

1) Services for offenders unite under specific aims and objectives;
2) Services can establish a common identity which ties those involved to a specific task;
3) A shared sense of purpose helps provide a consistent delivery of service;
4) A more coherent service can be developed by working to the strengths of the agencies involved;
5) The development of a single agency provides a stronger base from which policies can be developed and finances devolved. This enables services to respond more effectively to an identified local need;
6) A partnership can act as a catalyst for bringing staff together, developing a body of expertise and promoting new and imaginative ideas;
7) A partnership may develop initiatives beyond the range of a single agency, e.g., multi-agency training involving magistrates, the CPS, youth justice officers and local solicitors;
8) There is a much greater involvement in policy making committees by magistrates and the Judiciary;
9) The combination of agencies and resources means a more cost effective service, both financially and in terms of human resources.

However, there are common costs associated with these arrangements.

Costs

1) Being identified as an 'expert' service may lead to isolation from the parent agencies and the staff working in them;

2) The experience of being seconded to a separate agency may not always be positive for individuals not suited to working at a distance from the parent agency. The early return of seconded staff or resistance to the secondment package can be very disruptive;

3) The different conditions of service under which staff are seconded to multi-agency teams can make the development of a unified team difficult. For example, probation staff receive 36 days annual leave, social services receive a minimum of 20 and the voluntary sector lies somewhere between the two;

4) Voluntary bodies often withdraw once a project is underway. (This is largely due to intermediate treatment grants being fixed for 3 years.) This leaves the statutory agencies managing the service, possibly without the inspiration and innovation associated with the initial voluntary sector involvement;

5) Returning from secondment to a parent agency is not always easy, especially if newly developed skills are not required;

6) Individuals involved in the successful design or implementation of a working partnership may experience rivalry from those not so supportive of the new arrangements.

Chapter 9

Conclusion

Crime Wave or Moral Panic?
Young offending has been a major political issue since the Home Secretary's speech to the Conservative Party Conference in October 1992. At the time, most of the public debate and media coverage centred around the issue of persistent offenders and particular types of offence such as joy-riding.

The focus shifted in February 1993 after the appalling death of two-year-old James Bulger and the subsequent murder charges laid against two ten-year-old boys. Regrettably, much of the media coverage made this incident synonymous with juvenile offending as a whole.

In the same month, the House of Commons Home Affairs Committee Inquiry into Juvenile Offenders began hearing evidence. Although there were some substantial differences of opinion amongst those presenting evidence, it was clear that the recent changes in the law relating to juveniles and the shift away from the use of custody for young people was having a positive effect.

This discussion can therefore ill afford to confuse the issues of persistent offending and serious offending, or to take place on the assumption that we are in the midst of a juvenile crime wave which can only be solved by the introduction of draconian custodial penalties.

The declining number of known offenders
During the 1980s, there was a steady decline in the number of juveniles who were known offenders. These are young people who, having admitted guilt, are cautioned by the police or are found guilty by the court. Home Office figures reveal a reduction of 37% for the 10–17 age group, spread evenly across the various categories of offence.

Known Offenders aged 14–17 years, 1980–1990

Year	Male	Female	Total
1980	144,000	31,700	175,700
1985	139,600	36,000	175,600
1990	88,600	22,200	110,800

It is important to understand why this decline has occurred. Demographic factors do not provide an explanation. The biggest reduction in offending is in the 10–13 age group in which there was no fall in population between 1985 and 1991. The overall juvenile population did fall by 19% between 1980 and 1990 but that still does not match the decline in the number of known offenders.

The most likely explanation is that the changes in policing and sentencing policy discussed throughout this book served to reduce the number of known offenders. In particular, the increased use of informal and formal cautioning by the police and the use of non-custodial remand and sentencing options by the courts meant that fewer teenagers were exposed to the damaging consequences of imprisonment and the subsequent likelihood of re-offending.

The nature of young offending
While all criminal behaviour needs to be addressed, most young offenders are not committing serious crimes. A large proportion of offences are opportunistic and very few involve violent attacks upon the person. Although some have serious consequences, many begin as pranks or reckless adolescent behaviour.

Home Office figures show that in 1990, 81% of 10–17 year-old offenders were convicted for property offences and 10% for offences involving violence. Moreover, the number convicted for violent offences in 1985 fell by 4% from 19,200 to 18,500 in 1991.

Known Offenders aged 10–17 years, 1981–91 (1000s)

Indictable Offences	Males			Females		
	1981	1985	1991	1981	1985	1991
Violence against the person	13.3	12.8	11.6	2.0	2.5	3.2
Sexual offences	2.6	2.4	1.8	0.0	0.0	0.0
Burglary	41.4	36.7	20.8	2.0	1.7	1.4
Robbery	1.3	1.4	1.7	0.1	0.1	0.2
Theft & handling	102.2	105.2	57.4	30.7	34.7	21.9
Fraud & forgery	2.2	2.2	1.7	0.8	0.8	0.7
Criminal damage	5.7	5.8	4.0	0.4	0.4	0.4
Drug offences	0.8	1.4	5.5	0.1	0.2	0.6
Other (excluding motoring offences)	2.3	2.1	3.7	0.2	0.1	0.3
Motoring offences	3.9	2.7	0.7	0.1	0.1	0.0
	175.5	172.7	108.9	36.4	40.6	28.7
Summary (excluding motoring)	55.2	46.5	40.1	5.7	4.4	4.9
All offences (excluding summary motoring)	230.7	219.2	149.0	42.1	45.0	33.6
Offending rate (per 100,000 population in age group)	7,500	7,700	5,900	1,400	1,700	1,400

Only a small minority of young offenders commit grave or violent criminal offences. This does not make such offences any less serious – but a sense of proportion is required. Section 53 of the Children and Young Persons Act 1933 provides the sentencing framework for these cases. Section 53(1) deals with homicide offences and covers children as young as 10 years old. Section 53(2) covers those who are 14 years and over who have committed offences for which an adult could receive a maximum penalty of 14 years or more.

Persons sentenced under S.53 CYPA 1933 by offence group in England & Wales

	Number of persons							
Offence group	1984	'85	'86	'87	'88	'89	'90	'91
S.53(2)								
Violence against the person	26	19	28	29	21	23	12	25
Sexual offences	13	11	18	11	16	16	23	13
Burglary	10	31	25	24	32	16	15	12
Robbery	36	60	69	68	84	44	52	45
Theft/handling	-	-	1	-	-	1	-	-
Criminal damage (arson)	12	27	15	17	20	14	21	7
Drug offences	-	-	-	1	2	-	-	-
Other	-	6	-	4	2	1	2	-
All offences	97	154	156	154	177	115	125	102
S.53(1)								
Murder/manslaughter	22	18	16	19	22	15	10	12

Those convicted under S.53(1) are normally placed by the Home Secretary in one of two special Department of Health secure Youth Treatment Centres.

Those convicted under S.53(2) are normally placed in local secure units if they are under 16 and a half. However, some 15-year-old boys do end up with older youths in Young Offender Institutions.

New laws are therefore not needed to deal with these young people. On the contrary, the issue that really needs addressing is whether this sort of punishment works.

A 1992 Home Office Research and Planning Unit study showed that prison is a less effective environment in which to place these young people. It concluded:

○ local authority homes provide better education and

training, a higher level of throughcare and more help and advice with detainees' problems;

o the cost of placement in community homes is between 30 and 100% greater that in Young Offender Institutions although this does not take into account the more intensive education provision in such places;

o although absconding rates are up to four times higher, offenders released from community homes are statistically less likely to be re-convicted after two years than those released from YOIs and the nature of their re-offending is less serious.

These findings support the view that care and attention to individual needs is the most effective means of reducing re-offending. However, the solution does not lie in re-locating young people into institutions which are effectively local authority prisons. It lies in broadening the existing range of community-based non-custodial options.

This should involve moving all but the most serious, violent offenders out of secure units. Many of the young people presently held in them have committed no criminal offence at all. Many of those sentenced under S.53 are already in open conditions. The Home Office gave evidence to the Home Affairs Select Committee explaining that on 6 November 1992:

Of the 146 young people (not in prison) subject to S.53 orders, 50 were placed with the Youth Treatment Service in open conditions and 96 in Community Homes, 14 of them in open conditions . . .

The proven failure of approved schools
In October 1992, the Home Secretary stated in an address to the Metropolitan Police:

A small number of children are committing a large number of crimes. There is a case for increasing court powers to lock up, educate and train them for their own and everyone else's interest. We will certainly be taking a long hard look at the options which are available to the courts in dealing with serious offenders of this age. If court powers need to be strengthened or new institutions created, then they will be.

The end result of this 'long hard look' was the proposal to introduce a system of detention for 12–14 year olds similar to that which operated under the Approved School Order abolished by the Children and Young Persons Act 1969. At the time, it was realised that locking up such young children simply prepared them for lives of crime. A Home Office study published in 1975 showed that, over a five-year period, those leaving approved schools had a reconviction rate 49% higher than other offenders with similar characteristics and from similar backgrounds.

Despite this negative experience, the Criminal Justice Act 1982 paved the way for detention centres designed to provide a 'short, sharp, shock' for young offenders. Not surprisingly, the new detention centres merely repeated the experience of the 1960s. The Home Office Young Offenders Psychology Unit found that levels of re-offending remained the same as in normal centres: 75% re-convicted within two years.

It is difficult to see how the new 'get tough' proposals can offer a different outcome to the one above. However, they will be expensive. The government's current cost estimate for each place is £200,000 per child building costs and between £1,500 and £2,700 for weekly running costs.

Such large sums of money could be much more usefully used, for example, in building up a range of intermediate facilities including bail support schemes, fostering arrangements, hostels and half-way houses for vulnerable young people leaving care.

The Development of Non-Custodial Options
The positive shift towards non-custodial penalties experienced in the late 1980s and early 1990s did not taken place in a co-ordinated way. Individual counties and local authorities have taken some impressive initiatives but there has never been an overall government plan.

In 1983, the £15 million allocated for intensive treatment

programmes led to the establishment of 110 supervised activity schemes in 62 local authority areas. Some of these schemes survived to form the basis of existing programmes. Others operated successfully for 2–3 years before folding for lack of further funding. All were run by voluntary organisations in co-operation with Social Services.

This type of funding arrangement suited the government's wider agenda of breaking the monopoly of statutory agencies and local authorities over this type of work and restricting local authority spending. The responsibility for developing non-custodial alternatives became primarily local, leading to considerable regional variations.

It appears that in inner city areas, where the need for such programmes is arguably the highest, the competing demands for Social Services and welfare funding have seen juvenile justice services marginalised. This is not to say that a lot of hard work has not been done, but it is important to recognise weaknesses where they exist.

A further cause for concern is the lack of overall monitoring that seems to be taking place. Statistics are available for most schemes but often give different information. This makes regional comparisons difficult and clouds the possibility of a clear overview.

NACRO did receive government funding to monitor the results of the 1983 initiative. They found that:

- while the number of custodial sentences imposed on juveniles fell throughout the country, the fall was sharper in areas covered by the initiative projects. Between 1984 and 1988, the number of juveniles sentenced to custody fell by over 58% in the initiative areas and by 46% in other areas;
- the characteristics of young people sentenced to participate in these projects were similar to those of young people sentenced to custody in the same areas, suggesting that projects were achieving their target of catering for young people who were generally at risk of custody;
- the majority of juveniles successfully completed their

programmes and just 15% of juveniles attending these projects appeared in court for further offences (some of which will have been committed before entering the programmes).

o almost all the projects had an inter-agency management committee containing representatives of a range of statutory and voluntary organisations, and the majority of areas had established an executive committee with overall responsibility for the initiative in that area. Magistrates were members of 90% of the executive committees and 75% of the project management committees: their participation played a large part in ensuring the projects' credibility with the courts.

The Criminal Justice Act 1991 and the *National Standards for the Supervision of Offenders in the Community* provide the basic framework on which to expand this type of scheme. However, funding remains an important question that cannot be overlooked. Nationally, a long term, properly financed programme for the full development of non-custodial schemes must become a priority.

The need for an overall strategy

The changing nature of youth justice practice has come at a time when the social and economic pressures on young people have increased considerably.

While the broader crime prevention aspects of youth justice work have not been discussed in this book, it is clear that high youth unemployment, the limited access to benefits and cutbacks in youth and recreational facilities play a part in turning young people towards offending.

The Social Circumstances of Younger Offenders Under Supervision published by the Association of Chief Officers of Probation in 1993 focused on just this. The report, carried out by Gill and John Stewart in seven probation areas, looked at the social and economic backgrounds of 1,389 younger offenders (17, 20 and 23 year olds) under supervision. The study highlighted the high incidents of relationship break-up, the prevalence of local authority care, the types of crimes committed, levels of income

201

and their diverse variety of survival mechanisms.

Consolidating the shift towards non-custodial alternatives must therefore be part of a wider youth crime prevention strategy. The Howard League has outlined such a strategy elsewhere (*Young and in Trouble*, 1993) and hopes that this book offers some practical alternatives to the often counter-productive effects of institutional care and custodial penalties.

Non-custodial schemes are not offered as a quick-fix cure for juvenile offending. But they do offer an approach which places the needs of vulnerable individuals first and attempts to target the causes of the particular wrong-doing. At their worst, these schemes maintain the existing re-offending levels for custodial institutions while avoiding the physical and emotional risks inherent in custody. At their best, they offer an encouraging way forward for an age group which will generally grow out of crime and which responds to positive individual care.

References

Godson, D. and Mitchell C., *Bail Information Schemes in English Crown Courts*, London: Inner London Probation Service, 1991

Hood, R., *Race and Sentencing*, Oxford: Oxford University Press, 1992

Light, R. *et al*, *Car Theft: the Offenders' Perspective*, London: HMSO, Home Office Study No 130, 1993

Rutherford, A., *Growing Out of Crime*, 2nd edition, Winchester: Waterside Press, 1993

ACOP/NACRO, *Awaiting Trial*, London: NACRO, 1992

Stone, C., *Bail Information for the Crown Prosecution Service*, New York: Vera Institute of Justice, 1988

Thorpe, D. *et al*, *Out of Care. The Community Support of Young Offenders*, London: Allen and Unwin, 1980

Webb, B., and Laycock, G., *Tackling Car Crime: the Nature and Extent of the Problem*, Crime Prevention Paper No 32, London: Home Office, 1992

Legislation

The Children and Young Persons Act 1933
The Children and Young Persons Act 1969
The Powers of the Criminal Courts Act 1973
The Bail Act 1976
The Police and Criminal Evidence Act 1984
Criminal Justice Act 1988
The Children Act 1989
Criminal Justice Act 1991
Criminal Justice Act 1993

White Paper, *Crime, Justice and Protecting the Public*, CM965, London: HMSO, 1990
Green Paper, *Punishment, Custody and the Community*, CM966, London: HMSO, 1990

About the Howard League

The Howard League was established in 1866, the year that the first Royal Commission on Capital Punishment brought out its report which abolished public executions. Leading philanthropists decided to set up an organisation which would work for prison and penal reform as well as continue to press for abolition of the death penalty. It was called the Howard Association, after John Howard who had been the first prison reformer. In 1921 this organisation merged with the Penal Reform League to become the Howard League for Penal Reform.

The Howard League cherishes its independence. It has never accepted any government funding, and relies entirely on voluntary contributions from individuals and trusts, and income from subscriptions and events.

The core of the work involves investigating and commentating on penal policy and practice. The Howard League commissions original research on the penal system which is published in the form of books and reports. Occasional papers and briefings appear from time to time as well as fact-sheets which are regularly up dated.

Since the 1920s the *Howard Journal of Criminal Justice* has been published quarterly and provides rigorous academic analysis. The membership magazine keeps supporters informed of the League's activities and concerns.

Over the years the League has achieved many changes. It continued the campaign to abolish capital punishment, led the campaign to abolish corporal punishments, and helped establish probation.

The League runs vigorous public education campaigns:

- *Children in prison.* The Howard League believes that 15-year-old boys and girls are too young to be locked up in prisons. They can be managed effectively in the community using the wide range of schemes available. We absolutely oppose the new secure training centres for children aged 12, 13 and 14
- *Suicides in prison.* The Howard League was the first to raise the issue of people committing suicide in prisons. The League has conducted research, published reports and fact-sheets, held

conferences and meetings with MPs and Ministers, and kept in contact with the families.

o *Over-use of prison.* The League believes overcrowding is a symptom of a more profound problem:too many people are sent to prison on remand and under sentence. It is not possible, or desirable, to build our way out of this. We should reduce the use of prison in the first place. The League examined who goes to prison, published fact-sheets on imprisonment for debt and other trivial offences and raised it in Parliament.

o *Developing alternatives.* Most people can be managed effectively in the community. The Howard League works closely alongside probation, social services, police, magistrates and voluntary agencies to encourage the development of alternatives.

o *Prisoners' families.* Children and families have a right to keep in close contact, and this gives prisoners the best chance of resettling. The League produced the first ever guide to visiting prisons for families and held 10 workshops inside prisons to open them up to the community and families. The League published a report called *Families Matter* which generated a great deal of local media coverage. As a result, many prisons are improving their visiting facilities.

The Howard League's many activities include:

o Original research on a wide range of issues of public concern: commercial prisons, mothers behind bars, prison conditions, racial discrimination, foreign nationals in prison, are just a few recent examples. The League also publishes briefings on legislation, and sets up working groups to consider aspects of penal policy and practice.

o Conferences for professionals and anyone interested in the criminal justice system, on issues like young people and crime, race, violence, minorities and European prisons. The League holds a conference in New College, Oxford, every year on a major theme of national concern which lasts three days, and often organises one-day or evening events.

o A public information service, for schools, students, the media and MPs. The League publishes fact-sheets on 30 different topics, a video and teachers' notes on the prison system, booklets and briefings.

o Political briefing. The League works closely with politicians by providing factual information and holding fringe meetings at the national conferences. Members meet with Ministers, MPs and Peers and are asked to appear before Parliamentary Select Committees to discuss the League's concerns.

o The Howard League was one of the first voluntary agencies to be granted consultative status with the United Nations. The League participates in international debates and conferences, advising on penal reform worldwide. The Howard League's international committee monitors how the UK conforms to United Nations human rights standards on penal matters.

The UK sends a greater number of people to prison than any other country in Europe, yet our crime rate remains high. It is obvious to the Howard League that the over use of prison is part of the crime problem, not a solution to it.

Prison numbers. Each year 19,000 people are sent to prison for not paying a fine.

In 1994 the prison population stood at 48,000, having risen by 16% in 10 months. During the 1980s the prison population had always been high, dropping briefly during 1992.

15% of male and 23% of female prisoners describe themselves as black or Asian.

Over 73% of the people sentenced to immediate imprisonment in 1992 were convicted of non-violent offences.

25% of the people in prison are on remand.

58% of the people sent to prison on remand will not get a prison sentence or are found not guilty.

Costs. It costs an average of £442 per week to keep someone in prison. It costs £106,000 to build each new prison place, and £620 million is being spent on building new prisons. Community sanctions are much cheaper, averaging £27 per week.

Prison does not work. 50% of men and 34% of women released from prison are re-convicted of another offence within two years. This rises to more than 70% of youngsters.

Prison conditions. Prison conditions vary. As the numbers of people are being sent to prison rises, there is overcrowding and a strain on buildings and staff. The Chief Inspector of Prisons said of Cardiff prison: 'Cockroaches, rats and birds and other vermin were flourishing. A night visit to the kitchen revealed cooked and uncooked foods and the remains of the lunchtime meal left uncovered. All this marked lethargy and bad management.'

Young people in prison. Each year 20,000 young people aged 17 to 20 are sent to prison on remand. 57% of these young men, and 71% of the young women, will not subsequently get a prison sentence.

Average sentence lengths have increased from 9 months to 12 months in six years, and for young women from 6 months to 13 months.

31 teenagers have committed suicide in prisons in the last 5 years.

4,000 young people are sent to prison each year for defaulting on fines.

1,600 boys and girls aged 15 and 16 are sentenced to prison each year.

Prison suicides. 387 people have taken their own lives in prisons during the last 10 years. Each year the prison service records almost 3,000 incidents of attempted suicide and self-mutilation, about half involving teenagers. Three 15-year-old boys have committed suicide in prisons.

Mothers. About 6,000 women are sent to prison on remand or under sentence each year, and half of them are mothers. The Howard League estimates that about 6,150 children are forcibly separated from their imprisoned mothers every year.

The Howard League has published a wide range of research papers and reports on these and many other penal issues.

This book is part of a continuing commitment to raise public awareness and discussion around penal issues.

The Howard League hopes that the book will contribute to informed public debate and that readers will get in touch directly with the League should they want to know more about its work or its concerns. As a voluntary agency, the Howard League relies entirely on the goodwill and support of individuals and organisations. It has a growing list of donors and supporters, and new recruits are welcomed.

Frances Crook
Director of the Howard League
1994